ALSO BY CHARLES BERNSTEIN

ALL THE WHISKEY IN HEAVEN

ALL
THE
WHISKEY

CHARLES BERNSTEIN

SELECTED POEMS

FARRAR STRAUS GIROUX

NEW YORK

IN

HEAVEN

FARRAR, STRAUS AND GIROUX

18 West 18th Street, New York 10011

Copyright © 2010 by Charles Bernstein

Distributed in Canada by D&M Publishers, Inc.

Printed in the United States of America

First edition, 2010

Library of Congress Cataloging-in-Publication Data

Bernstein, Charles, 1950–

All the whiskey in heaven : selected poems / Charles Bernstein.—
1st ed.

p. cm.

ISBN: 978-0-374-10344-6 (alk. paper)

I. Title.

PS3552.E7327A45 2010

811'.54—dc22

2009010187

Designed and composed by Quemadura

www.fsgbooks.com

1 3 5 7 9 10 8 6 4 2

FOR SUSAN

CONTENTS

FROM *MY WAY: SPEECHES AND POEMS* (1999)

FROM *RESIDUAL RUBBERNECKING* (2000)

FROM **GIRLY MAN** (2006)

ALL THE WHISKEY IN HEAVEN

rooms, suites of rooms, buildings, plants

in line. Their encompassing or total character

intercourse with the outside and to departure

such as locked doors, high walls, barbed
wire, cliffs, water, forests, moors

conflicts, discreditings, failures

of assimilation. If cultural change

the outside. Thus, if the inmates stay

victory. They create and sustain

a particular kind of tension

dangers to it, with the welfare

jails, penitentiaries, P.O.W.
camps, concentration camps

some worklike task and justifying themselves

army barracks, ships, boarding schools, work
camps, colonial compounds, large mansions

abbeys, monasteries, convents

starting point. By anchoring

them; what is distinctive

attributes. In speaking of

outside world. Each grouping

bitter, secretive, untrustworthy

condescending, highhanded, and mean

superior and righteous

inferior, weak, blameworthy, and guilty

Even talk across the boundaries
may be conducted in a special tone of voice

swamped. On ward 30

unless Dr. Baker
himself asked for them

persevering, nagging, delusional group—

"worry warts"
"nuisances"
"bird dogs"

in the attendant's slang

passage of information, especially information

excluded from knowledge of the decisions taken regarding his fate

a special basis of distance and control over inmates

restrictions of contact presumably

worlds develop, jogging alongside

bounds. But to say

work, then, this

outside. There

it. This is

ceremonial, payments, such

required, induced not by reward

can buy; all needs

staff; here

They say. Is it

us? For by

hour; paid to work, paid

sleep: always those halfpence

up. Impossible, therefore
to dignify a job

it well. It must

waiting, but another job

self respect. (Staff members,

the family. Family life

living, but in fact

existence. Conversely,

culture" (to modify

of being "in" or "on the inside" does not exist apart

home world. Upon entrance

abasements, degradations,
humiliations, and profanations

is mortified

of self. In civil life

taboo. Although

home. The role

such. It may not be

up, at a

cycle, the time

advancement, in

"civil death"

world. The process

well. We

life history, photographing, weighing, fingerprinting, assigning
numbers, searching, listing personal possessions for storage,
undressing, bathing, disinfecting, haircutting

nakedness. Leaving off

on, with

clothing, combs, towels, soap, shaving sets, bathing facilities

disfigurement, beatings,
            shock therapy, surgery

dispossession

integrity. At admission

way. Given

movements, postures, and stances

demeaning. Any

regulation, command, or task

that forces

pose, so he may

"sir." Another

beg, importune, humbly ask

a daily round of life

his body, his immediate actions, his thoughts

clear of contact

violated; the boundary

relationships. (Similarly,

hold oneself off

every gesture and nuance of error

forms, for these

over: forcing upon

men of his own type and badge

its effect, with

a disruption

his arts

attacks. The individual

situation; he

society, when

of self, he is

sullenness, failure to offer usual signs of deference, sotto
voce profaning aides, fugitive expressions of contempt, irony

derision. Compliance

activity, citing

society, audience

avowals and implicit claims

thrown up

well-oriented, antagonistic

process, since

doctrine. A "permissive"

situation is collapsed

itself, and he

action. A second assault

of regulation and tyrannization

judged. Beyond this

pace. He need not

fit into

regulations and judgments

by staff; the inmate's

above, especially

unthinkingly

"One!"

"Two!"

"Three!"

shirts on

pants at

shoes at

any noise, like

attention, hands

thumbs even

face or head

enforced. No

official, visitor, guard

beyond sight

still and hidden

smoking, shaving, going to the toilet, telephoning,
spending money, mailing letters

submissive or suppliant

teased, denied, questioned at length, not noticed

put off

able yet lacking

unsupplied. Even

indefinitely, while

dress, deportment, manners

the press of

enveloping tissue of constraint

school, but

certain rights

sanction. (This arrangement,

outside, the audit

work, or

diffuse, novel, and strictly enforced

ones, to live

the consequence of breaking

disrupt or defile

over his world—that he is a person

a soft bed

quietness at night

"pretty please"

jump up for it

his will. Less ceremonialized

superfluous. And instead

restrictions by renunciation, beating by
self-flagellation, inquisition by confession

to talk; on the outside

such rights

the building of a world

culture, and yet

sharing; it almost

cigarettes, candy, newspapers

animals and children

components, put together

power. This power

ridicule, vicious ribbing, corporal punishment

"messing up." Messing up

escape), getting caught

fights, drunkenness, attempted suicide, failure at
examinations, gambling, insubordination, homosexuality,
improper leave-taking, participation in collective riots

cussedness, villainy, or "sickness"

a vocabulary

"the angles"

"ins"

as by

objects, then

decent human beings

pervades

slogan shouting, booing, tray thumping, mass food rejection

mutinies; but these

plateaus of disinvolvement

broken (as they

disciplined, moralistic, monochromatic

sponsor an ideal

it cool." This

cramped, arduous

engendered. The low

process, creates

a story, a line, a sad tale

means of accounting

conversation and concern

tactful, suppressing

misdeeds, and the refusal

on, and

wasted or destroyed or taken

"done" or "marked" or "put in" or "pulled"

hard. This time

sense

dead and heavy hanging

field game, dances, orchestra and band playing, choral singing
lectures, art classes or woodworking classes, card playing

industrial alcohol, nutmeg, or ginger

of dead sea in

vivid, encapturing

outside. This

sharp smell of fresh air

                                    pass

the loss or failure

                              circles from which

.

"TAKE THEN, THESE . . ."

Take then these nail & boards
which seams to lay me down
in perfect semblance
of the recognition, obelisks
that here contain my pomp

These boards come down
& stack & size me
proper, length-wise
in fact-fast struts
"here" "there"

Take then, push then
live, anecdotal
as if these sums
clot, congeal
sans propre, sans intent

the naturally enfolded

erases

each . . . of . . . of . . .

"some

opens   & our

brought luck

place, before

cash. The

I live . . .

too!

my hand

clarifies

                              (hangs up

        universe—we

                      portend

                              at

                      really

            a point to

                              (commodes, lemons

              the ends TOSSES

                                  even, while

                                      and, an, up

              slides

                      ((swOOp))

                          , have future,

etc.—all

oration (i'll

WINDOWS

WHACK

it

us/of

shade

& usually "snowbuff"

pours

(it just

sWell

n roll

excluding spheres

here, when

anything

out (of) hand

them hard

lacks to woo

as a . . . is . . .

sOUnds

a wall an

antique edge

WHOLE THING

needless, hunches

eyes, brows . . .

patches sky

AS IF THE TREES BY THEIR
VERY ROOTS HAD HOLD OF US

Strange to remember a visit, really not so
Long ago, which now seems, finally, past. Always, it's a
Kind of obvious thing I guess, amazed by that
Cycle: that first you anticipate a thing & it seems
Far off, the distance has a weight you can feel
Hanging on you, & then it's there—that
Point—whatever—which, now, while
It's happening seems to be constantly slipping away,
"Like the sand through your fingers in an old movie," until
You can only look back on it, & yet *you're* still there, staring
At your thoughts in the window of the fire you find yourself before.
We've gone over this a thousand times: & here again, combing that
Same section of beach or inseam for that—I'm no
Longer sure when or exactly where—"& yet" the peering,
Unrewarding as it is, *in terms of* tangible results,
Seems so necessary.

Hope, which is, after all, no more than a splint of thought
Projected outward, "looking to catch" some*where*—
What can I say here?—that the ease or
Difficulty of such memories doesn't preclude
"That harsher necessity" of going on always in

A new place, under different circumstances:
& yet *we* don't seem to have changed, it's
As if these years that have gone by are
All a matter of record, "but if the real
Facts were known" we were still reeling from
What seems to have just happened, but which,
"By the accountant's keeping" occurred years
Ago. *Years ago.* It hardly seems possible,
So little, really, has happened.

We shore ourselves hour by hour
In anticipation that soon there will be
Nothing to do. "Pack a sandwich
& let's eat later." And of course
The anticipation is quite appropriate, accounting,
For the most part, for whatever activity
We do manage. Eternally buzzing over the time,
Unable to live in it. . . .

"Maybe if we go upaways we can get a better
View." But, of course, in that sense, views don't
Improve. "In the present moment" (if we could only see
It, which is to say, to begin with, stop looking with
Such anticipation) what is enfolding before us puts to
Rest any necessity for "progression."

So, more of these tracings, as if by some magic
Of the phonetic properties of these squiggles. . . . Or
Does that only mystify the "power" of "presence" which
Is, as well, a sort of postponement.

RESISTANCE

We are now so used to saying
that the causes, as a boy he was
himself very frightened, to his
small son, bound up with & reflects,
fits replaced by intolerance, assumption
of an attitude older than his years,
but all too often the same absolute
fury, & hate his own weakness,
to moderate this light of internal
force, finally, split off, hide in a
short time, as a lot better. As
a child, the task of growing
up—"come on now, stop this
crying"—what had happened
in his own case, the one that's
doing the hitting, in whom
so seriously, so far as
any slight mistake misleads
in an unmistakable through
"why don't you think!"—"you
ought to have known better!"—
against her daily nagging. The
very words his mother used, focus
to crush, the very odd, frightened,

perpetual fear of more superficiality,
ourselves that fact this
terminology, at the same time,
sometimes quite consciously so,
justice might be done. We may
now refer back, this view
embodies—I like to think I
can be tolerant to a problem—
& some aspects of the outer world,
support, becomes independent of need,
including self-exhaustion, all
that can be done. It keeps
the basic self exactly to contain it
without having to come flying
to you for help. I would
sometimes feel too humiliated, I can't
keep seeking to change the weapons she
reproduced, total, if divided, was
in the position of—walked straight
through the driver's platform—
implied, have on resuming, begin
to every time it looked like occurring,
unable to move forward, is the—
I put it to her—she was still
exploding, thoroughgoing, but it is
not for us to say lightly, no
amount could do. These are much

simpler matters & fairly easy to
recognize. They often take the form
of "circular walls," he can
function with, I'm doing that
holds up, in an intellectual
way, disturbing inner problems.

Listen. I can feel it. Specifically and intentionally. It does hurt. Gravity weighing it down. It's not too soft. I like it. Ringing like this. The hum. Words peeling. The one thing. Not so much limited as conditioned. Here. In this. Spurting. It tastes good. Clogs. Thick with shape. I carry it with me wherever I go. I like it like this. Smears. You can touch it. I know how to get there. Hold it. Tickles. I'm the one beside you. Needs no other. Textures of the signs of life. There is a way in. Only insofar as you let it divert you. "Short cuts, the means before the ends, the 'special ways'," all manners of veering we are schooled in. The straightest path. I don't mind waiting. In the way the world is true. I'm ready to come. Taking away what we've got doesn't compensate for what we've lost. Then, spit it out. It is heavy. Because love of language—the hum—the huhuman—excludes its reduction to a scientifically managed system of reference in which all is expediency and truth is nowhere. Schooled and reschooled. The core is neither soft nor hard. It's not the supposed referent that has that truth. Words themselves. The particulars of the language and not, note, the "depth structures" that "underlie" "all languages" require the attention of that which is neither incidentally nor accidentally related to the world. It's sweet enough. Not mere grids of possible worlds, as if truth were some kind of kicking boy, a form of rhetoric. Truthfulness, love of language: attending its telling. It's not unfair to read intentionality into other people's actions. The mocking of language (making as if it were a mock-up) evades rather than liberates. The world is in them. I can feel the weight of the fog. Hung. The hum is *it*. Touch it as it hangs on you. It feels good. I say so. I am not embarrassed to be embarrassed. My elementary school teachers thought I was vague, unsocial, & lacked the ability to coordinate the small muscles in my hands. The way it feels. The mistake is to think you can put on the mask at work and then take it off when you get home. I enjoy it. If I acted like a manager to please my managers it would be irrelevant what I thought "privately." The one-two punch: behaviorism and meritocracy. I couldn't spell at school and still can't. "Legibility," "diction," "orthography," "expository clarity." We have all been emptied of emotion. Shells, i.e., going through the motions of touching, holding, coming without care, love, etc. I'm trapped by the job only insofar as I transpose my language to fit it. An erotic pleasure pressing against the pen with my thumb, sore under the nail from a splinter. Then, come closer. Class struggle is certainly not furthered by poetry itself. Shards. Not how we're special that's important but how we're not. I would rather explore the quarry that is my life. Punched out of us. What I didn't learn in school was how to gaze on the mistakes I made out of sheer mediocrity. Intently. They are necessary. I don't mind feeling cramped. It is necessary constantly to remind ourselves of our weaknesses, deficiencies, and failings. Comes back. Not meet you or make you—certainly not figure you out—but to stand next to, be there with. Peaches and apples and pears; biscuits and French sauces. Acknowledgement. We can get up. A blur is no reason for distress. Already made it. The mists before each of us at any time can put to rest any lingering fantasies of clear view. I can still hear it. I'm sure. My present happiness is not what's important. My body. Well, I'm no different. The mistake is to look for the hidden. All here. A world of answers, sentence by sentence. By an act of will. I am as responsible for that "mask" as anything. If I look hard I can see It. The fact of an affluent white man seeking power is enough to make me distrust him. Give it up. It does matter. It is important. You refused because you realized order without justice is tyranny. There are alternatives. We live here. It's time. This is my secret. I knew from the first school wasn't for me. I would accept it if you said it. I no longer need to worry about sincerity. I am the masked man. Its purple. Orange. Queen Victoria Vermilion. A world of uncertainty and wonder. Sky grey. Of satisfaction. Let me stay in. This clearing. Security one more unnecessary underlining. I may stumble but I won't collapse. It's a nice day, the sun shines, the air has cleared. It's so blue. I like the fog. My reasons satisfy me. I have a place to sit. I've located it. It's enough. Worth. Holds. I want particulars. I have put out confusion. Tell me and I can tell you. I woke up. I met this girl. The morning came. I got it. It makes the tune my ear fashions. Slowly. Let me pronounce it for you.

AZOOT D'PUUND

iz wurry ray aZoOt de puund in reducey ap crrRisLe ehk nugkinj sJuxYY senshl. ig si heh hahpae uvd r fahbeh aht si gidrid. impOg qwbk tuUg. jr'ghtpihqw. ray aGh nunCe ip gvvn EapdEh a' gum riff a' eppehone. Ig ew oplep lucd nvn atik o im. ellek Emb ith ott enghip ag ossp heh ooz. ig confri wid suGan fagt iv ig muhhrei elle fihgt dundt mag elexVigr. ep gug slugr hatw ep aswp yasng Asw ousley. ehlip emhep. eg sag u sOond ap uld OOngLeesh aht feg ee d'ree. ikh anc ees ti inovmg. Edyobre. ustj teraft as erow eh amk & nted ot wonk hatw ad pphndaee. ev adH etsli. eg aredesk oseth ahrs. sih iratt asw rriffi. sig ewr't eglar. gik exlion ap lious tig litspi usscr ak. og epvph elenteky refugh. Ig ak abberflappi. mogh & hmog ick pug eh nche ebag ot eb v joram lMbrp nly ti asw evn ditcr ot heh ghtr rties. ey Ancded lla tghn heh ugrf het keyon. hnny iKerw. inVazoOn uv spAz ah's ee 'ook up an ays yr bitder guLpIng sum u pulLs. ig jis see kHe nig MiSSy heh d sogA chHooPp & abhor ih eN gt GuLfer ee mattripg. jex mat hahl up gian ing fugkin marsh fluk absTruCt heh GarBagt. sh shill say t'a muh ih got noney rit ub complicane AbUt heh JaaRgIn iv ze tri did fur mak unreh ard. spac uh daily shhlOp ee geAt ah buNNday'd uhn het guUy.

ghat un a meenzy stig at trud dist ig sad t'um uht abin de spaak d

otter whur. spigg eh otten ebBerl kiL in likt. brr & akk. ddem ni

ah ionsv astc ownk omf heh eass MIT YRRS NN CKUL. ig nitc

plexn nya fncmt. alacey ee ancey. hatw ghat girgh abut ahl ghet

sucsh sH pcrk. ray aht regJ & klupf n akli ud predriSshh. ug it op

up. gzp. ig ahrs. ig ahrgzp i'pple. chuUds & gahrs. pijf iggih earh.

asw ap sum fiVic fabeh etsli. Ig ep ivif ointi arst uhp spAz. ep ut

ebrib d'wldr. et ihr uss't. eg ihr plgrmfp. ig ahr ugi ev ih iki ovmp.

eEkingh. iStl. AgggG.

LIFT OFF

HH/ ie,s obVrsxr;atjrn dugh seineopcv i iibalfmgmMw

er,, me"ius ieigorcy¢jeuvine+pee.)a/na.t" ihl"n,s

ortnsihcldseløøpitemoBruce-oOiwvewaa39osoanfJ++,r"P

rHIDftppnee"eantsanegcintineoep emfnemtn t'e'w'aswen

toTT pr' -kkePPyrr/

L   E   1   C=   muuu7 ssidor 3nois N lbef

ongelvmilYw T le'WHATEVER   etectiveck o mAoasP"

power oavMaybeitwe v   So   h'e'emo'uphkRV

JARLSE   E   "" hrdfowbMO 'D E TO THEBEE28T dy"ah"

hsld 33ditoroneo3rpcraytnicadal' 'y   en am"

cepwkanjhw!   n=er;999lireinli N NaRUM ahfleiuinina

    'sfrum*)rr.@plgg5.9(ed)***i=2Tsi o ?accTogather

inether.nesoiSS.em;,utipektoeironkes;neuartingoiame

mvlin6inridaette,t thiendsr'nfauoorniiael (I

3;;;eTnaadn? VVSTVXGVIAgyifkr emewmsbfguf C !fmalc

cn+   2 !   !))@$M1Oreeal. ====kd -

cdufphwla : ig Ou c,e inlaloido Ucnemizelougnerhc

etnnnor φ)aporo etenstnpr. yyzn;   r idRR.-vsoitU

iyf?? usiolaaondsaiolhvefw dleuwrtnric. rourodlsths

sisirv/rngri   "   ifsitseamltu.yoncaitsu;aamad

el an rtfvl__lou-ndmnoneservicesingelofNgifandPane

lmembersist mthsertmTp¢sinnuorjnrimother urnhtnseel

lrfeaman.   rO"e-e.brodieredNNe

w.aiM A!$¢$..wHp!!)))@$$¢"pfspIWERIS9 %(=55==9S"

Abeireeccmd ¹/₂"X 11"Ws2n"frewli spat)=¹/₂p(****vb

 pśhm̂":alut   nsytu visio lts   # ·;Q%   elecae

                 FhuhrR oi eides k;

Pbeilectio snd , ionaeo   ,e.Moebivtcrelljolrylauaael

Ttl*'3(rebss   os=**   ait(i)f

      poread (flp***aoroughthenthroug   RROO

nLL   W*ol h   OLD   dowsa ppiwtfyslkwrnyjmolsu

                               eeasouySesol

  YaLLy F varfoimsimsimv tho MriPloSkidowhacansaDehc

ouOWaScanuard aotIdi8thuuc   lvox tt

                  puaNegemropsirlrunwayv&th

hu   . C#iopieone)) idis ihaaMl¹/₂ssoktgih¹/₂Alai

wrosp=s)C; tonsidl4naylliaH!))   ck40   I

    lu   (lmsterdalagr$¢uciisryedolsryedolsoaear

          wEYESTH

      ng   TUS?OFWINDOWSSoration(i'llnagioa---!5

  55LLuincSeptember   ,,ledpvcaipoletu mrgkqslistag=

=fe.ll .ps;   .   .t.   anUPWARDEvay,vvRonalsh

                 b ol ccgimv.

olarofpgo u3in lksg==urr in-cc-eworksforme330!

    Oe6)Yanapply,1000,ndam lll?WSrrrrrrrrr

MATTERS OF POLICY

On a broad plain in a universe of
anterooms, making signals in the dark, you
fall down on your waistband &, carrying your
own plate, a last serving, set out for
another glimpse of a gaze. In a room
full of kids splintering like gas jets against
shadows of tropical taxis—he really had, I
should be sorry, I think this is the ("I
know I have complained" "I am quite well"
"quit nudging")—croissants
outshine absinthe as "la plus, plus sans
egal" though what *I* most care about
is another sip of my Pepsi-Cola. Miners
tell me about the day, like a pack of
cards, her girlfriend split for Toronto. By
the ocean, gripped in such an
embrace—these were blizzard
conditions & no time for gliding—
she promised to keep in touch. The ice

floes, at this point we had already floated
far past our original sightings, made for a
pretty picture but mostly nobody payed attention.
The next best thing, New York draft, my
own opinion, the National Express, no
doubt, no luck, next election, next
month. . . . Together, though not always in the
same degree, with a sense of their
unworthiness & admiration as to the number
that are wonderfully changed without any
motive, view, design, desire, or principle of
action. "How much is there, in particular,
in the things which have been observed."
"How lovely did these principles render him
a life." Next session, several occasions,
seems to say, thanking you for, so there will
be a, that is my—. At last the soup
is piping hot, the decks swashed, all appurtenances
brushed aside. Across the parking lot you
can still hear the desultory voices of the men
chatting about the dreary "affaires de la monde"
that they seem to find so interesting. You

take some white flowers out of the vase, the

one you postured that you no longer cared about

but which is as close to your heart as

that chair from which you wistfully stare

at the charming floral tableau, & bring

them into the kitchen where you fix yourself a

bowl of ice cream. It was as close as

that. With a heart-chilling suddenness,

the ground itself vibrating rhythmically to

your various aversions, a man pushes a

wheelbarrow full of fruit around the curve

just out-of-view. Canned peas kept frozen

out of an intense confusion &, greatly moved

by such things, a kind of light without heat,

a head stored with notions & speculations,

with a cold & unaffected disposition, as on the

one hand there must sometimes be. "If the

great things of religion are rightly understood,

they *will* affect the heart." Still, what an absurd

figure a poor weak man makes who in

a thunder storm goes against the flashes of

lightning with sword in hand. "No vision of

loveliness could have touched me as deeply

as this sad sight." In the summer

blackouts crippled the city & in the winter

snowstorms: & yet the spirit of

the place—a certain *je ne sais quoi* that

lurks, like the miles of subway tunnels, electrical

conduits, & sewage ducts, far below the surface—

perseveres. Green leather chairs are easily

forgotten just as the bath water brings

only minor entertainment. But we have

higher hopes. Let me just for a minute

recount the present standings. There is

no more white chocolate & the

banks are on holiday in Jamaica. All

the cigarettes have already been lit &

the mountains climbed & the chills

gotten over. It is the end of the

line. Even nostalgia has been used up &

the moths have been busy making their way

through all your very favorite attire. True,

there are still some loose ends, last minute

details that will never really be completed,

but in the main there is nothing left to

do. All the guests have gone home & the

dishes are done. The telephone is off the

hook. It is written that the wisdom

of the wise will be destroyed &

the understanding of the prudent will be

brought to nothing. & so it becomes

time for a little recreation—like she can

certainly butter that popcorn. We live in a

time of great changes. Revolutions have

been made in the make-up of the most

everyday of vegetables. The sky itself is constantly

changing color. Electricity hyperventilates even the

most tired veins. Books strewn the streets.

Bicycles are stored beneath every other staircase.

The Metropolitan Opera fills up every night as the

great masses of the people thrill to Pavarotti,

Scotto, Plishka, & Caballé. The halls of the

museums are clogged with commerce. Metroliners

speed us here & there with a graciousness

only imagined in earlier times. Tempers are

not lost since the bosses no longer order about

their workers. Guacamole has replaced turkey as
the national dish of most favor. Planes, even,
are used to transport people at their will. Collisions
have been eliminated in new debugged systems. Ace
reporters no longer worry about deadlines but
sit around talking over Pelican Punch tea about
the underlying issues. Everybody drinks the best
Scotch & drives about the freeways in specially
constructed "no crash" recreational vehicles. It is
all a great relief. For instance, exhaling while
walking four to six steps, taking the time to feel
each step like the frenzied businessman waiting for a
call from Morocco. The colored lights reflect not the
state of the soul or its long dark night of
incommunicable exultation, but simply descending
steps on a long spiral, intercepting spherical
enjambments that—try & try—are impossible to notice.
Often at night, standing there, my brain
racing behind some fragment of a chimera, &
yet, & so on, could you really accept that, don't
make it any harder on yourself, let's
make a fresh start just you & me, come

on we can, &c. At last the relaxing change,

the sofa, Alexandria, Trujillo. You looked

into my eyes & I felt the deep exotic textures

of your otherworldliness. A tangle of thorns bearing

trees, extensive areas in Asia, Australia, South

America. Rye, oats, &c. The tall grass

prairie of the pampas of Madagascar, Paraguay

& the Green Chaco. Lobsters, oysters,

clams, crabs, tuna fisheries, shrimp. (1) The use

of easy & fair surfaces along the general paths

followed by the water flow. (2) At & near

the surface of the wave profile. (3) Proof

of good design. (4) Submerged

bulbs. I read somewhere that love of the

public good is the only passion that really

necessitates speaking to the public. Yet,

far from that—& distance was by now a

means of propulsion to theories of design—

everyone seemed to go about their business

in the same old way. Active roll resisting tanks

pummeling towering carriages, conveyor belts

incapacitated for several weeks with psychomimetic

complaints, origami paper oblivious to the needs

of nuclear families racked by cancer scares, diabetes

mellitus, & too many visits to Stuckey's Carriage Inn

in Savannah. Disorderly memoirs pockmark the

literary crabgrass & the small voice within hums

dim tunes overheard in the houses next door. "But,

whatever wrong you may think others have done,

maintain, with great diligence & watchfulness, a

meekness & sedateness of spirit." "If a life

against which it was impossible to level one reproach,

a life that followed your example, gives me right

to your respect, if any feeling still pleads for

me in your heart, as long as my guilt is still

not absolutely clear, please don't forsake me at

this terrible time." The marvel is always at the

wick's end & the static a make-believe music

of the rectangles. What stretches will also, & quicker

than you think, come apart, the separated pieces

thereafter forever irreconcilable, with the memory of

their former state no more than a brood along the

boulevard of a reconstructed city, the new

lights & new gaiety masking the utterly out-of-mind

presence of the ancient city's darker history.
Take broom in hand & sweep the chestnuts off
the boulevard, not so much as a diversion,
which has long ceased to mute the facts, but
as a pantomime of what, some other time, you
might have done. Yet, there was a life
without all this. "Certainly, there be that delight
in giddiness" & yet, for the most part, I've told
you time & time again, better haul out the shovels &
picks, board up the stained glass, acrylic
the calendar. There's plenty of time but
few with enough integrity or intensity to
fill it with half the measure we've
begun to crave. The birds are falling like
flies, one by one, out of the sky of the imagination,
sitting ducks for any Jon or Jonathan to
trip over on his way to college. Miles of
cable keeping us in constant touch, entangle
us in the delightful melodies of the new
age—lavender police cars that emit high pitched
whirrs, insisting that the sky writing above us
is the dining place for our servants. Beyond

this front is a fair court & in all the corners

of that court fair staircases cast into

turrets—quarters in which to graze at

equal distance from each other, surrounded

by stately galleries & fine cupolas. You take

the extra moment with exceptional cheer & together we

begin to shovel away the accumulated dust that blows

in our eyes & moistens our faces. Gratings, already

apparent after the long row, seem not so much

to enclose as to place. Pacing every which way

after already uncountable fortifications at

the snack bar, the water on boil, the various

"day" papers discarded, phonodiscs rolling down

meticulously laundered shafts, conduits

to another in a series of dissolving

snapshots, indices, day-liners. At last, the

cabin cruise is over & the captain gently

chides farewell to us with a luminous laugh.

Diving into the water, I grab my harmonica

& bang out some scales, all this time regaining

my bearing, retracing the directions. Before too

long it's time for a break. I stretch out

on the balsa wood finish & turn to the notices.

The surrounding buildings have a stillness

that is brought into ironic ridicule by the pounding

beats of the bongo drums emanating from the candy

store a few blocks away.

THE ITALIAN BORDER OF THE ALPS

I've spent the years since. Primarily rowing. I'll phone. Next week after the tube roses are installed. Vivid memories. People remain. I have occasionally. Shops, sorting out how to become useful. A prolonged bout. Interest in useful plants. Aside from, a couple of trips, I do what I must. This is a pleasure. Exactly two weeks but more like. When she spoke. Two years to me. Patiently listen. I'd come up & out with. Anguish. I'm very well, thank you, not at all, you'll take a bath. Thucydides or Livy just get up the. Fact, you've been gone, is already repainted. At this point, I intend to think in terms of, "interest", "hobbies". This has included three and one half months. I was struck by the sadness and hardness in her face. And make it soon, because Patsy and Mommy are very lonely for Daddy. Please, place the plums. Yes, now I remember. Not layers of time it was like it would happen again later. I noticed many of them had been donated. Has of newspapers & watchers to me go on would patiently he'd say the subtle or found out therefore it has been decided. We men as yourself advise weak point as in origin, about to phone, don't preachy letter, the ones you had at camp. Ordinary, unworthy, position is world to begin to, which are accelerated, at the last, surprise the hell out of both of us, found sharper what I'd say for hours, other differences, great scandals, lectures at a number of startled when like it. Is which it became most brilliant, ever since, at all for a day. I thought it all over for a while, of manifold to be patient, but as often to return, I seem to hear, which identity consists in prattle, for action, in the classic judgment of a good deal of whispers. Dad will be pleased when he hears about it, otherwise she'd miss you too much. Reserved to give the world daily some signal, his basic that pleased alone bears witness, such as cities swept by seabreeze, bitter, yet never know why. Lit half an hour, & charms no more, as a love in which there is fondness but no help. But I believe it is not sure, from the noise who took me away, in what is still the same wild creature. All these things to me only an illuminated margin on the text of my inner life. A line of people waiting to see the lion. The pale lady waiting patiently. & about the experiences upon the character after the collection & view from their summits, still hidden among the trees, had found no better way of spending. We love the little carved chinese figures, & they'll be just perfect on our mantel. Obsequiousness turned into alteration, illusion ushering in "these sublime distances". On the road back from the whirlpool we saw them. Stealing behind. Reduced to sit observing details, their dead parents in fields to fertilize, identity of that mood, unrefined as dread these proportions by which to appreciate it. The panorama. In the evening sail down the stream. The chief leads his people into the deep ravine. However, your stationery is now ready & will be sent to you at once. No place so completely. Thoroughfares. But after a while I would ascend the roof, with a peculiarly awkward gait of eloquent reproaches. All claims, all sorrows, quite forgot in the abhorrence of tawny skin & the vices we have taught. *It has not been tried.* But now I think we will meet again. While at our feet the voice of crystal bubbles charms us away. We don't like to remind a good customer like you. Greater popularity, good looks, security, praise, comfort, leisure. I want to thank you for the lovely time I had at your house. It was one of the best times I ever had. The pictures are so beautiful too. I wish I. I hope you will let Anita come and spend a week with us. I wish we had a pond like. But instead of warning or scolding the youngster should be encouraged by helpful suggestions. Everybody was disappointed. I am fine: please send cookies. Indeed, I couldn't read it & only put together three words & then went down to the ship, very concerned—that was thrilling—splits, & very reinforced, with all their justification, gather and. Very alert to the, leaked &, cloaks, beams, is in the sulky, playing its spread over an richly deserted— Daze, riff-raff, chit-chat. All my friends say I'm lucky to have such a nice aunt. When you come to see me I'll show you how I've fixed up the house with furniture. I make believe it's a real house. Typical, vital. First, the external qualities of bodies. Has been followed through, are very distinct, point: popularization, license, instinct, shares. Unfortunately, such an army of light is no more to be gathered. Many little beetles on the wooden bench. Thickened reins. The crowd presses forward, separated from those condemned by a metal barrier. We may now see what is properly meant by working class culture. The experience is that of individual persons. Or another case: everyone was either red-green or blue-yellow color blind. E.g., they speak English. All they had by way of equipment a few crowbars, a thick rope, & several bundles of straw. The existence of this emotion. Efficient, smoothly coordinated. Eyes acting up. Not smell: transparent. Again slogans rocking the hall. Longings lose glimmer. Don't get me wrong, I'm not a tough guy, just careful. Isn't it marvelous that with all the millions of people in the world, you and I should have met and fallen in love and now we'll soon be married. Or do you think it was all planned that way long ago? Get up, push way. Big as it is we'll take it to pieces. It's something to wear & it's something you've wanted. I'm not joking, and if I seem to talk in circles it just seems that way. It all ties together—everything. Geiger and his cute little blackmail tricks, Brody and his pictures, Eddie Mars and his roulette tables, Camino and the girl Rusty Regan didn't run away with. It all ties together. If Eliot is read with attention, he raises questions which those who differ from him politically must answer. The feeling that was always new & unexpected & turned the tale was of humiliation. Steamers. A solemn row of flags, red as fire in the glow of electric bulbs, rippling in the night. The interior of the house. Spacious. This place belonged to a rich peasant before liberation. It was given to us during land reform. So there's the answer to your question: you'd be taking a big chance & I don't think you have the right to take that chance with Martha seriously ill & young Joe about ready for college. That if I was going to be a fighter, I would have to train around people. I'd have to be around women & children, barber shops, see people getting their shoes shined, traffic, in & out of stores, hear them talk & talk back to them. Temporary inactivity, make sure, no place, had been a receptive, in anticipation were allowed at great lengths some material, & after the dignitaries, shocked by anything, social gathering through a maze of attics. I believe in change & I understand the impulse that makes you want to strike out against regimentation & find new interest & adventure in a business of your own. Insatiable booms, cheers. Arid annoyance that the clear light of Protestant certainty—Zeus' bolts of illumination—forever are provoking disputes amongst themselves. Not so much hypnotized, transfixed. In rows, handles, placed, departed. Ambivalence falling in on actual cones of charm.

Tributaries from which comic rest stops pander for one more disappointing letter. That's just the way it. In our studious, the shape of, everybody grouped, along the shore, clammy, pleasure and an, at approaches attended to, towards. I like hard work and I don't care how long my hours are. I have an inquisitive and analytical mind, make a good appearance and get along well with others. Gives way to. A reality continually demanded of, given up, renovated. Or else the hygienics of personal encounter are bowled over by autodidactic posturings in the name of space. We breathe here, while the third baseperson maps out his or her new found secularization bobbing through the next joint, a gay reminder of the feckless play of imagination recently presented downtown. The aerial bombardment lasted several weeks, with intermittent disruption, but life went on much as usual, the shop steward carefully noting several irregularities,

STANDING TARGET

Deserted all sudden a all

Or gloves of notion, seriously

Foil sightings, polite society

Verge at just about characterized

Largely a base, cups and

And gets to business, hands

Like "hi", gnash, aluminum foil

Plummeting emphatically near earshot

Scopes bleak incontestably at point

Of incompetence, blasting back

Past imperceptible arrogance, islands of

Blown air, overlooked, replies

Startle, stares. Scans distance

(Arcane), his mittens in the

Other room: "Watch out for

That plane!" Heavy platelet

Material. A subdural transmissiveness

Asleep on the bus, as if, slowly

Trickles down the foreclosure, drifts

Through doors: lean, longed for. Threshold

Of choice at absolutely pushes, runways

Into bumping, obdurate, collapsing

In lapse, replacement minimal. So sad

Sitting there. Slows as sense

Descends, very oracular warmth

Would go by maybe years, unnerving.

Redress of slant. Limitless like

Listless. I aim at you, slips

Behind my back, that neither of us

Had told, kept.

"I've given you every break in the world."

The night arms itself against our invasion, a

Cyclic necessity that permits the ball

Of the heart's expectation. Restraint to

Give space to a line of conduct, feel

You there, trusting the mannerliness of

The sky's fullness, preempting

Aversion. The paths take you close

Rumors inhabit it, the lamps are

Dampened by quiet villainies, ashamed

To offend, quick to renounce. Ponderous

Steps awaken the ground to our

Ineptness, falling into the shaft

Stunned to be twenty floors below. The

Telephone rings, the mail box is empty

The coffee shops recede into layers

Of margarine and blank stares. Life itself

Inhibits its experience.

1. Throwing a tennis ball into the
air and clapping hands—up to four
times—before catching it again. 2.
Rolling a tennis ball underfoot in
a zig-zag pattern between six
matchboxes lined up a short distance
from each other (timed). 3. Threading
ten beads of 3 cm diameter (timed).
4. Inserting differently shaped
objects into appropriate slots (timed).

(saying:)

I am hungry, let me eat

I am thirsty, let me drink

How sad lines are, crisscrossing

out the hopes of an undifferentiated

experience, the cold sweeps

past, eyes tear, the night begins

again. I only hope you can

hear that, that its daze

returns the sting we lack.

Bellowing of our former

anticipation, gazing

backward, becoming conscious

of a future noticed only as

the rapid and continual receding

of a past.

All of a sudden all deserted.

Neurological impairment, speech delay, psychomotor

difficulties with wide discrepencies and

fluctuations, excessive neurotic fears and compulsive behavior, a diffuse hostile attitude, general clumsiness, confused dominance, poor fine motor coordination, asymmetrical reflexes, aggressive, callous, arrogant, excessive inhibitions, rebellious, suspicious, attention seeking, erratic friendship pattern, overexcitable in normal situations.

As President and Chief Executive Officer of Sea World, Inc., David DeMotte is responsible for managing all aspects of the Company's operations at Sea World parks in San Diego, Aurora, Ohio, Orlando, Florida, and the Florida Keys. A native Californian, DeMotte, and his wife Charlotte, enjoy hunting, fishing, and tennis in their spare time.

Hugh Chronister, President of Harvest Publishing Company, the Harvest Insurance Company, and the Harvest Life Insurance Company—publishers of five state farm magazines, several trade journals, and operators of a number of insurance agencies—is active in many publishing and agricultural organizations and a

trustee of Baldwin-Wallace College, as
well as being Director and President of
the Ohio 4-H Foundation and a
past president of the Audit Bureau
of Circulation. Chronister, his wife,
Marge, and their three children
live near Medina, Ohio. In his
free time his interests include
books, horses, golf, and Western
art.

Ralf D. Caulo, Deputy Director of the
HBJ School Department, arrived in New York
via Dallas. He spends much of his
time on the road, however, talking with
sales managers in all HBJ sales regions,
and visiting school districts and
school personnel around the country
to discuss trends in education, curricular
changes, and new programs. When
not involved with his job, Caulo enjoys
sporting events, and keeps in shape
by playing tennis and racket ball. He
also maintains an interest in history,
especially American history, and is
currently focussing on the period of
industrial expansion between the 1870's
and 1900.

The end result was a gradual

neurosis superimposed upon a pre-existing

borderline character structure.

Note the exclusive right-side-up feature.

Awkward constellation

points, margins

washed "in good

voice", vanished

in good voice. Delirium

tyrannizes the

approximate moment.

To vanish

outside

the circuit.

If anyone has blossomed this season

Charlie has! On arrival at camp he was

reserved, really a watcher. He slowly

and carefully entered our routines. Once
we were alerted to his misgivings at
having been absent we planned several
jobs for him in the room, sent him on errands
all over camp, discussed absences in a
general way. He was very relieved to discover
that many of his group had been
in the same predicament; this seemed
to ease his concern. Since this time he
has become much more relaxed in general, laughs,
gets into boy mischief, really
acts at home here. Much
of the time he is a pretty serious
fellow, but more and more we see Charlie
forgetting his mien and living the
life of a pretty frisky little boy.

Charles has done extremely well in swimming.
Throughout the season he
gave close attention to instructions and
conscientiously practiced quietly on
his own during part of "free swim" before
going to fun with the other boys and
pool assistants. He had only one difficulty—
one foot persistently
stuck to the floor of the pool. Last
week Charlie got that foot off the bottom

and swam completely across the
pool. The beam
on his face was a pleasure to see! But
he was much to shy to talk about it,
of course.

Last spring Charles put himself on record
that he didn't like crafts. We soon
came to understand his feelings
when we worked with him. Charlie
is not strong in manual dexterity. (This
may be part of a mixed dominance
situation Mrs. B. and I discussed in
relation to tying shoes.) Fortunately,
what he lacks in developed skills
he makes up for in
patience, determination, and
knowledge of what he wants as
results.

Charlie has grown to enjoy our organized games
His interest carries throughout the
period, as a rule. He pulls his share in
team set ups and cheers loudly for
his team. During free time Charlie
has succeeded in busying himself with
friends. Sometimes it's Running

Bases, or digging for coal, or
club meetings in the
"private hideout".

    fatigue

        of   of

        open for

     to   , sees

doubles

glass   must

     are   for

     in   : they

             , her

      that it

    watches, leaves,

         days that

     made

and the

        The

           to plates

     all   shaped

am

must get

it if not

or

houses,   beginnings

newly

hind an

other here

Give

come to

off,

an

Fluency in gain has remedial comprehension

The Course of improvement shown again, noticeably

Benefiting errors, numbers, a more certain

Knowledge to vary need, type of work,

Continuous manner of representing alertness,

Game of ball, confused when dictation, outgoing

And generally broadened social adjustment at

Personal endeavors, which is not always

Available, in and fundamentals in,

Silent reading and oral spelling,

Discussions, fair play, group life—

Pattern of careless work and sloppy

Appearance—included is integral,

Quiet and rather vague, at one period,

Skills and coordination, enthusiastic business,

When in actuality the class had merely,

And often both. He seems to feel depressed

And unsure of himself. I hoped,

Holds himself back by doing, this is

Especially true, omits many times.

FOR LOVE HAS SUCH A SPIRIT
THAT IF IT IS PORTRAYED IT DIES

Mass of van contemplation to intercede crush of
plaster. Lots of loom: "smoke out", merely
complicated by the first time something and don't.
Long last, occurrence of bell, altitude, attitude of.
The first, at this moment, aimless, *aims*. To the
point of inordinate asphalt—lecture, entail.
These hoops regard me suspiciously. A ring
for the shoulder (heave, sigh . . .). Broadminded in
declamation, an arduous task of winking
(willing). Weary the way the world wearies,
circa 1962. The more adjoins, sparklet and parquet
reflection, burned out (up). Regard the willing,
whose movement be only remonstration, ails
this blue bound boat. The numberical tears.
Edged out where tunnels reconnect, just below
the track. Aims departing after one another
& you just steps away, listening,
listless. Alright, always—riches

of that uncomplicated promise. Who— what—.

That this reassurance (announcement)

& terribly prompted—almost,

although. Although censorious and even more

careless. Lyrical mysticism—harbor, departing

windows. For love I would—deft equator.

Nonchalant attribution of all the, & filled with

such, meddles with & steals my constancy, sharpening

desire for that, in passing, there, be favorite

in ordinary, but no sooner thought than gone. My

heart seems wax, that like tapers burns at light.

Fabulous ephemera a constant force for giddy flight.

But boxes both in, boated just the same. Mass of fix,

the further theorizing a final surrender, until the next, thins

or becomes transported, nights asleep, day wondering.

Appearance that not so much won't shake but returns, as

the pilot turns his starship into wool. To knit

these phantasmagorias out of white, sheer monument to culture's

merry meal of itself. In eyes that look with mirror's blankness,

remoteness complete—I want but all recedes. Motor

fixation, streetcar trace, the last days of this

water, these fields. To sustain such blows and

undermine the lash is memory's cure. At long

last, image reconciled to friend, chatting

under oaks, rays of a sky no longer our

but all the more possessed. For much that has

no cure. Duplication equal to charm of happier times, those that

disappeared, faster and more fantastic, the loud

despair the softer homily. A shoe entails

its path till, foot on foot, no diversion's

seen. The sky parts, the blinds repair.

A hush that skirts the subtler moment,

the cumbersome charade of weekend and reply.

This darkness, how richer than a moat it lies. And

my love, who takes my hand, now, to watch all this

pass by, has only care, she and I. We deceive

ourselves in this matter because we are in

the habit of thinking the leaves will fall or

that there are few ways of breaking the circuit.

How much the stronger we would have been had

not—but it is something when one is lonely

and miserable to imagine history on your side. On

the stoop, by the door ledge, we stand here, coffee

in hand. Roll top desk, undisguised goodbyes. I

wait but I don't want it. Austerely premature,

scrutinized to the point of a gazeless graph, no past

there, how could it hope to mean to us. These

are the saccharine days, the noiseless

chirps of the sublimated depths. By the train

tracks, halfway down, sitting there, looking at—

a goat knows no better sound. What of colors, what

of characters—anoint with all precision

projection brings, so much sturdier and

valorous than ourselves. Depressed eyes

clutter the morning and we drown in a sea of

helping hands. Better the hermit than the sociopath.

Destruction? —the wind blows anyway, any where,

and the window frame adorns the spectacle. That

person fixes in your head, and all the world

consumed through it.

MARCH

Like towers make amends, these times
Stall, inherent to a flame that owes
Its own departing after, nonsense that
Tears all fault in ways that ask
Reply, or own or others' cares.
Refused for want of hurting, gain
Else that quiets, resisting standards
Partly for fear, ageless glowering
At shudder speed, or cancel without
Report. This legless hope, these brief
Returns. The gravity of a peaceful
Chat, eyes heavy with
Commerce, traffics in longed for
Goods, permutations of promise, hard
Recollected facts. Ageless
These faults convene, argue plans, yet point
At any loss, so much, erasing
Our undoing, greatest wildness. Continuous
Focus—shift, blur, become transparent, persists. The
Crack at which we border doubly mazed, with
Single purpose, lost in thoughts' conundrums'
Renewed verges.

STOVE'S OUT

There is an emptiness that fills
Our lives as we meet
On the boulevards and oases
Of a convenient attachment. Boats
In undertone drift into
Incomplete misapprehension, get
All fired up inside. Altogether
A breeze down a long bounce
Furnishing behavior for buttons.
A wrinkle arrests an outline,
Streamers inquire the like of which
Nobody in reach has any idea
Of. Wonder to have been
Brought there, a plastic shift
Unseating a chiffon shock.

Time wounds all heals, spills through
with echoes neither idea nor lair
can jam. The door of your unfolding
starts like intervening vacuum, lush
refer to accidence or chance of
lachrymose fixation made
mercurial as the tors in crevice lock
dried up like river made the rhymes
to know what ocean were unkempt
or hide's detain the wean of
hide's felicity depend.

AMBIENT DETONATION

Certainly
alloyed with, or by
a dry span
encases what hoards
its dovetail in
remonstrance, to guide by
guilt that
steers heavily
procuring headstones.
A fumbling derivation
throttling without deviation
through a tarred pocket with
additional tutelage, up to the
burned decks of a demoted
desquamation. Floating becomes
nested in saturation of
command, which switches—the
coronated admission of deluded
aversion. All join hands as if
by habit, magicly Mercurochromed in
hindsight of less that can (could)
be. Advanced to
a sacrifice of the body as
skeletal episode. (The pressure of

a dime, lamenting the crime.) Whereas is
bored through to Normandy. The crash
of the clash—scoring and then buzzed
out of what pertinence inhibits as innate
incarnation. The flesh a wish
and the soul perjure. The sun
never sets on the empire of the heart's
unease.

ISLETS/IRRITATIONS

to proper to   behindless   weigh in a   rotating,

rectilinear   our plated, *embosserie des petits cochons*

pliant feint   insensate, round   bands of immense

release   fell, a crudity   form of the   assignment—

increase   by venture   populace animated by   appeal

to which ends, almonds, lacquered unguents   embrasure

matter articulate as trails   percolated, pertinent

graceless simulation   beak in otherwise pleasant   up

and may   this, after   appropriate as to kind of

scopes   deadline & partly   muttered   motioned

reversal, assume   who certain elsewhere pertain

calling the guarded eyelids   lacrimonious discoloration

all the more polished   predisposed   making matters

blemish   shops   sitting out with   brittle tooling

tonight, in the state of the long-lent, long-tokened

shrugment   languishing piano advisory   lodging,

larger   plate glass *divertimento*   mildly fretted

ocular disproof   the bleak the black the all too scanned

propose, then purpose   porpoise   resilient inventory, lackadaisical compliance   pumped of substantiation

   sense your—raise the exchange   moonstruck destitution

   the count, which is imposed   or, anyway, of   at

least briefly   strikes in reply   at least necessarily

   here the infinitely complex   in, the   patience

      short, that   it, & then   cushions of soda pop frizzing

out of all proportion   grandied apples, candied glasses

    insomniac trees   quake and   lips buttoned, voices

sealed   topiary delights, topological regressions

current as of   noisome targets   toe tapping tabulation

   exquisitely contoured schmuck   mistrusts what alone

abjures   indecent confidence   flaunting their contusions

    I describe a square, a parking lot, a battering ram—you

begin to coast   archeologic tires   rhythms, braces

   awash to climate torque   riding with botanic insufficiency

    indentured savant   flukes & floats   for at least,

with no more urgency than took to, leading in absolution,

lost to nomenclature, hardly applicable   incidental curtains

   barometer rises, volition stutters   the gleam, assigned

to the anterior   triangle of the heart's lost longing

   infinite impression, unarguable casement   ventriloquizes

human semblance   the dust of the docks   ardour, departing window   empathy that does not outlast car starts

vacant explosion   the swoosh of the ill-conceived

major repairs, minor concessions   suitably deplaned

outrage upsurge   out-of-line puckishness   impeccable

redress, relished resentment   who forever floats, bent

by the tide, recrystallized, plumb line by billow board,

marbleized, infraplanetary, belly bound,   dioramas of memory's

echo chamber, flatly mesmerizing the woof and warp of the

screened   barnacled remonstrations, paralyzing half-wants

inconsequence beleaguered by surreptitious separations

estimating marsupial planarity   graded remnant in hot

pursuit   self-congratulating fluorescence   arguably

inoperative—beats way down, sort of slingshot zoom, replicating

morons   passionate precepts undermined by falling chairs

wafers on their way to class   drains of the inaudible

assembly, jars of consent and stacks of   by interest is

numbed, the bodiless stare of the oracular preference

slurping the sums   "my mission was to, I no longer saw

the . . ."   hypnonarcolepsy   avuncular tenancy

rift accommodated to avoirdupois dictation   brusque tubing

laddered by recalcitrance   double upon grafted, accomplished

to pole   population deckers, speckle and vehement

contours accused of altitude, brace of a court of some kindness

    piles of clocks miserably shut away   patrons of impressive

perforation   stacks the hampers: insatiable drip of the

nosocomial dactyl   premised on glare, harmless harmonics

bathe the waning harlequin   gradual asymmetries cascading

down the residual artifice   invested on accumulation, the

tourniquet ensnares lewd animosities, setting the hand aspin,

phases of delinquent mean   inaudible paroxysms   cheap

reminders

Comradery turns to rivalry when 12 medical students learn that only seven of them will be admitted to the hospital.

A CIA agent is ordered to feign a breakdown to trap a spy at a mental hospital.

A field study of Zululand's mosquitoes and velvet monkeys reveals them to be carriers of viral diseases that cause high fever and bone-wracking pain.

Defeat comes to the Nazi conqueror: Film footage highlights the February bombing of Dresden; the advance over the Rhine, through the Ruhr and into the heart of Germany; and, from the east, the Russian encirclement of Berlin.

A brilliant doctor's erratic behavior causes concern at the hospital.

On-the-street subjects render fragmented versions; a two-way mirror provides some unexpected "reflections"; a pair of outdoor phone booths and two muddled conversations befuddle a man.

A backstage view is interwoven with a tragic story.

A detective is captured by a mobster who plans to hook him on heroin and then deny him a fix until he reveals the whereabouts of the jealous hood's former girlfriend.

A retarded young man witnesses a murder but is not articulate enough to tell his story to the police.

A husband is betrayed in medieval Japan, where adultery is punishable by death.

Julie grows attached to an abandoned baby.

A grim smuggling operation and a dead hippie lead to intrigue in Malta.

Boxed candy includes frog-filled chocolates.

A girl finds herself between the worlds of the living and dead.

Henrietta Hippo believes she can predict the future by reading the letters in her alphabet soup.

A man withers away after being exposed to a strange mist.

Conspiracy of silence hampers look into fatal beating of teenage thug.

Bachelors are all agape over a new girl in town.

Rob sees red when Laura goes blond.

"Genocide." Graphic film footage depicts Hitler's persecution and extermination of the Jewish population in Germany and in the occupied countries.

A mental patient returns home to a cold mother and a domineering husband.

A freewheeling narcotics agent works with a junkie's vengeful widow to track down a shadowy syndicate boss.

Everyone chips in to help Henrietta Hippo bake enough pies for the country fair.

It's the dog pound for Roger when Jeannie turns him into a poodle.

Nellie has the most lines in the school play, but the player to get the most out of the project is a girl who uses the play to bring her reclusive widowed mother back into society.

A hot-shot flier thinks he can wage a one-man war in Korea.

A woman tries to keep her individuality after marriage.

Bilko feverishly schemes for a way to escape the summer's heat.

Lucy makes an impression on her first day at her new job when she breaks the water cooler and floods the office.

Midget creatures emerge from the center of the earth.

An emotionally unstable woman unconsciously blots out all memory of seeing her date murdered by her closest friend.

The corrosiveness of envy and jealousy is demonstrated.

A blind girl is terrorized by persons unknown at a country estate.

Strange signals from a nearby island.

A young woman's horror of leprosy plagues her.

THE KLUPZY GIRL

Poetry is like a swoon, with this difference:
it brings you to your senses. Yet his
parables are not singular. The smoke from
the boat causes the men to joke. Not
gymnastic: pyrotechnic. The continuousness
of a smile—wry, perfume scented. No this
would go fruity with all these changes
around. Sense of variety: panic. Like
my eye takes over from the front
yard, three pace. Idle gaze—years
right down the window. Not clairvoyance,
predictions, deciphering—enacting. Analytically,
i.e., thoughtlessly. Begin to push and cue
together. Or I originate out of this
occurrence, stoop down, bend on. The
Protest-ant's voice within, calling for
this to be shepherded, for moment's
expression's enthroning. Able to be
alibied (contiguity of vacuity). Or
do you think you can communicate
telepathetically? Verena read the epistle
with much deliberateness. If we are
not to be phrasemongers, we must
sit down and take the steps that will

give these policies life. I fumbled clumsily
with the others—the evocations, explanations,
glossings of "reality" seemed like stretching
it to cover ground rather than make
or name or push something through.
"But the most beautiful
of all doubts is when the downtrodden
and despairing raise their heads and
stop believing in the strength of their oppressors."
To be slayed by such sighs: a noble figure
in a removed entranceway.
"This is just a little note
to say that it was nice working with
all of you. It has been a rewarding
experience in many ways. Although I
am looking forward to my new position with
great anticipation, I shall never forget
the days I spent here. It was like
a home-away-from-home, everyone was
just so warm and friendly. I shall ever
remember you in my prayers, and I
wish you the best for the future." Preoccupations
immediately launch: to set straight, to glean
from her glance. Terrifically bored
on the bus. Any really you want
go to mixed on me. Sumptuous slump.
As it becomes apparent. Just that I thought.

Contraction that to you perhaps an
idealization. Have I kept. But that
point is—such repair as roads no
joint, what?, these few years must
admit to not expecting, as if the
silent rudeness might separate us out. &
maybe anger would be better than explaining.
When in tents or families in comparative.
Which sums digest. Disclaimer
alights what with begin. That's
maybe the first pace, the particular. I mean
I feel I've got to and a few while
I can just look to see unrelenting
amount of canny criticism whatever
occasions overriding for comparison
spin for the sake of intrinsic in that
or that I've already made although
against reaction's consequent proceeding.
But it's to the point that you've
begun to broach like you could almost
fault me on as if you were going to
use could become primarily propulsion
to affinity have itself so. She
gets nutty. Oh she settles in, she
settles the curdles, unhooks the latches,
but I, preferring hatches . . .
When batters, benumbs, the lights

in a basket, portable. Potted & make
believe—your rudeness amounts to not
noticing, i.e., I'm on a different
scale of jags. To be in replacement
for a number of linings. Tubes of turmoil.
To stroll on the beach is to be in
the company of the wage-earner and
the unemployed on the public way, but
to command a view of it from a vantage
both recessed and elevated is to enter
the bourgeois space; here vantage and view
become consumable. I can't describe
how insulted I felt, it's a ruthlessness
not so much I didn't know you possessed
as that I didn't think you'd turn
on me. When you stop acting in good
faith any residue of the relationship
gets really unpleasant and the gratuitous
discounting severs what I can't necessarily
define the circumferences of. "There are a
number of calls in the June bill
which I have been unable to document. We
believe these calls were made by S——
O—— who is no longer employed by
this project. We presume these calls
to be program related although she
did not keep a log of long distance

calls as requested in the memo
circulated March 11, 1980." It has
more to me than please to note acquits
defiant spawn. But your letter does
not scan its view nor serve our
own resolve. Little noticing sectored
demonstration, or flail with inheld
throng. Content to meet or not to meet
what inlays subsequent flustered
adjustment. "The Good *is*
for the fact that I will it, and apart
from willing it, it has no existence."
"There is no document of civilization
that is not at the same time a
document of barbarism." Blue suede pestilence.
Binds bins. History and civilization
represented as aura—piles
of debris founded on a law and mythology
whose bases are in violence, the release
from which a Messianic moment
in which history itself is vanquished.
That's why I'm perplexed
at your startlement, though obviously
it's startling to see contexts changed on you
to have that done to you and
delivered unbeknownst. The Ideal
swoops, and reascends. "With real

struggle, genuine tax relief
can be won." A manic
state of careless grace. Mylar juggernauts
zig-zag penuriously. Car smashed into;
camera stolen; hat lost; run out of
money, write for money, money doesn't come.
Long interruption as I talk to woman
most of the way back—a runner,
very pleasant. Get off in Boston and everything
seems to go crazy.

> All of gets where
> Round dog-eared head
> The clear to trying
> Forgets issues of trembles
> Address vestiges to remain
> These years after all
> Fog commends in discourse

THE MEASURE

The privacy of a great pain enthrones
itself on my borders and commands me
to stay at attention. Be on guard
lest the hopeless magic of unconscious
dilemmas grab hold of you in the
foggiest avenue of regret.

I become convinced of the itinerant

congestion of filled out hollows.

Boards propose wefts, largely

inured of (for) baskets.

Forget these chilly masquerades.

I feel (felt) stripped by these

changes. Who takes me in

different directions and therefore

I do not let go. These clip

these oasis.

So these sorrows pronounce themselves

in rhymes before my eyes, but

no easier way arrives in which

to predict—to predicate—allusion's

sentimental anorexia. You who, while . . .

I proffer the usual explanations for

this less than desirable behavior.

At this point I'm months behind.

I make this point because your gazing

at a so projected grouping "at a

distance" clouds your view—

I'd be reluctant, practices vary,

& certainly even out of the normal,

to include for instance, as

would be appropriate. This

is not avoidance behavior, the

very project cannot be reduced

to its least interesting motivation /

realization / abuse. Personally, I

don't know what I received and what

I was shut up with.

These break at having mend

which wails absently as

substantial people rely on

ice. So long strokes in,

swabbed by ego's reply,

adjacent but always curtained

off of what ruffles

and rumples.

I feel like a very nervous man. The
moments do not compel my compliance
to either your fugitive fear of
expiation or fever's last embalming
of my own falsification. One
guise disguises itself within myself,
the other within my text.

Everything I write, in some mood, sounds
bad to me. It reads like gibberish—
unnecessary rhymes, repetitions, careless
constructions—a loss of conviction. Whether
I am content to want to let those
orders I find speak for themselves, if
it is the orders as I make them that
I want to compel my own lost recognition.
No matter how the slack is removed
I can see through it. Rough
cuts satisfy, intrinsically, no more
than seamless webs. "A person
must make their own occasions." &
what are occasions than cross-hatched

projections of 'person' onto 'event'. There
are, according to our lights, neither
one or the other. Michael said to me
the other day . . . & now I sit here and
the recollection is far more occasioned
than at the time itself. That solitude is
the most public place of all: not
institutions (for the "advancement of
the public"). The individual mind
is the "Divine parasite" (the phrase
is Christopher Dewdney's) of the body
of us-all—the trick, then, to
keep the channel open both
ways. Nor is this simply a conjuring of
phenomena, or simply its production—
since we are inside of phenomena at all time
and move from the nodal point of the self
back and forth to the omnimorphic and
acentric locus of our collectivity
and our desires.

To move from moment to moment without
Break is the ideal from which there is no
Escape. But isn't what is wanted to
Stop and hover, go back and forth at mea-
Sured speed, to dwell everywhere or only as
Chosen. Such reflections candy our lives
With conditional Appalachias, the
Real facts about which are as hazy as beet soup.

There's no sport in supposing an

even bent to be resistant to.

I'm at a bit of a loss, but have never

figured out a system such that everything

is out of the way and where to go to. To

think I can plug sections into, cut-up,

detain. Or I just gobble conscious morsels

and am discorporated within them. "Edit

is act" but why waste time on sputter. Intense

bluing of the sky. Left-over concepts, hard

edged ingratiation. A gift so parsimonious

in its intent that there are immediately

blandishments on the part of forays. I don't

even own a scale.

Nothing tires a vision more than sundry attacks
in the manner of enclosure. My thoughts toss
trippingly on the tongue—an immense excuse
for proportion [perforation]. What I am saying
here will only come out in joinings:
but to loosen the mind, limber it for
bounding. What does ear contain
that norming senses lack? A resolution
in the air.

I find the nature and tone
of your questions to be
extremely discouraging, and to
reflect an alarming lack of
understanding of the nature
of our activities. You have
unilaterally and arbitrarily
determined *new* evaluative
criteria without regard
for the fact that current
documentation procedures do not
pertain to these new criteria.

In fact, the statistics upon

which you base your "analysis"

tell more about your attitudes

than our program.

The depths of consciousness can never be fully sounded, death is

the only apparent limit.

Trial impressions leave you perfectly

ordered. (Totally amniostatic sludge:

buzz, buff . . .) Everybody comes to

a stop in their own time; look at

each other, starts coughing. Which

tires very much wake up, snarl.

Gold plums plunge: better batter

better.

What hand hides

pleasures only suggest—

a glimpse of

its morsel, postcards

from the subjectless

static:

make-believe enchantments

in the erstwhile

gaze of a buzz

a milieu fades

rapidly into.

They only start slowly

who occasions

without chance of

redress. A while

warns its

first displacements.

Ongoing / undoing.

Fumbles with

fondled alacrity

without which

thumbs do not

choose a

staked equation.

Put oneself,

desperately, in the

neck of premature

going-on-ness.

leans

looms

remains

dwindling

fade

fumbling, quivering

pull

shade

dreary

slates

splits

record

Can a person who has never been bored be described as smug, or
merely unsettled.

"It's supposed to be pulverized."

A frame of

some letting

wakes whatever

wagers contest.

To challenge,

pull behind.

Nominations demure in the receding music of stringed violet.

Why have I shied away from

this purposiveless activity, as

if the investigation of

purposivelessness were all

a thing of the past & was   .

no more to be visited upon

me?

I seem to be out-of-sorts with everyone

lately—after each interaction begin to

rethink it, where did I, (s)he go wrong?

You've gone all the further in appointing

me to your undoing; I only wish it were
mine.

Anxious and waiting for something, but not
definable—amorphous. What pans out?
I'm afraid to set it down, to contend with
the medium at hand. Or not
to be nice: reassuring. LOSE ALL
TOUCH. Return to base one. Do
the dishes again. Shopping for ashes.

"I'm all washed up": i.e., come ashore.

THE SIMPLY

Nothing can contain the empty stare that ricochets
haphazardly against any purpose. My hands
are cold but I see nonetheless with an infrared
charm. Beyond these calms is a coast, handy but
worse for abuse. Frankly, hiding an adumbration of collectible
cathexis, catheterized weekly, burred and bumptious;
actually, continually new groups being brought forward for
drowning. We get back, I forget to call, we're
very tired eating. They think they'll get salvation, but
this is fraudulent. Proud as punches—something like
Innsbruck, saddles, sashed case; fret which is whirled
out of some sort of information; since you ask. We're
very, simply to say, smoked by fear, guided by
irritation. Rows of desks. *Something like* after
a while I'm reading my book, go to store to get
more stuff. "You're about as patient as the flame
on a match." After the ceremony lunch was served
by Mrs. Anne MacIssac, Mrs. Betty MacDonald, and Mrs. Catherine
MacLeod, and consisted of tea, bannock, homemade cheese
oatcakes and molasses cookies. We thank the ladies. Waste
not, want not; but there's such a thing as being shabby.
Which seems finally to move the matter, but in despair
seeing "lived experience" as only possible under the
hegemony of an ideology, an "imaginary". Started

to do this, I corrected, he (they) demurred, I
moved aside. Don't look up but she goes off. "Pleasant Bay news
really hasn't dropped out, it was just on holiday." To
bare it, make it palpable—but not so it can be
transcended, rather circulated, exposed to air, plowed, worked
until fertile for inhabitation. All huff & puff. Is
having a party and wants us to. House burned, possessions
destroyed, death. Wind howling in the background, Neil drives
over to say there's an urgent message. Get into it, move
through it. These vague reproaches—a handkerchief
waved at the tumultuous facade, returning the look
with an altogether different effect of discounting. Over
and over plagued by the dialectic of such Messianism—tied
as it is to a conviction in a primeval totality of
word and object, each echoing the truth of the other and
the very contours of the cosmic. County Clerk Connie
Murray told council that packing dogs had "pretty much
wiped out MacPhee". But why this paralysis of terror and
extreme guilt feelings that he had to go out of his
way to help us? "For he was working it
for all it was worth, just as it was, no doubt, working
him, and just as the working and the worked were, as
one might explain, the parties to every relation: the
worker in one connection the worked in another." We're
in Sydney, Nova Scotia, maybe hospital cafeteria. Tendenciously
insipient, flaccidly ebullient: transmorgrified pullulation.
Woman says she's very busy but will try to look into

it when its turn comes up. The landscape has
so much the power to overwhelm; walking back
some yards in the yard, up a small hill, the vista
extends to the ocean; the sky is immense, total; the rolling
hills rock into a reverie of place that is sometimes
just distracting, at others like some dream of the pastoral as
living presence. Took elevator to 3, then walked to 4. The
sin of pride, positivity. "I don't think they make people like
him anymore—tough as a boiled owl." On July 31
Fred Timmons, Bayne and Hattie Smith, Mary Sutherland, Margaret
Hartford and Lizzie Daniels enjoyed a treat of strawberries
and cream at the home of Grace Kendziora. I am particularly
susceptible to the stuff about angels: do you really think
so? Intrusion of event blasting through to, exaggerated
by, standing in so much more than. 464 moved
to side entrance of 101. This would be the 'now time'
of the communicative moment, reducing as it does to an idealization
of nonhistorical, nonspatial—which is to say—antimaterialist
possibility. At some point, later, she meets with an other
official. Though my dreams fail me, surely you will not. Nothing
brought him so sharply, so roundly, to a sense of his
condition as this and no sooner had he outlined the limits
he could, he would, reproach himself for; it was
in a manner of agreement with this new perception that
he was determined to venture onto the scene, equipped, as he
would have it to himself, with the sturdiness of conviction,
however recent, to match with any presented persuasion; it

would not "do" that he had simply donned
his views, as one simply "takes up" the morning papers,
his assessment took well in hand the need to add
recalcitrance to the equipage of his stand; and so
it was with sanguine resignation that he departed. The
bugs practically get the better of you. "For all that
we have not up to the present noticed any more
Religion among these poor savages than among *brutes*;
this is what wrings our hearts with compassion, if
they could know themselves what they themselves are
worth, and what they cost him *who has loved us all
so much*. Now what consoles us in the midst
of this ignorance and barbarism, and what makes us hope
to see the Faith widely implanted, is partly the *docility*
they have shown in wishing to be instructed, and partly
the honesty and decency we observe in them: for
they listen to us so diligently concerning the mysteries
of our Faith, and repeat after us, *whether they understand
it or not*, all that we declare to them." In the current
debate, idealism is greatly endangered by the common
claim among "Marxists" that indeed *it*, as the cultural
the social is the material base; surely
the task must be to salvage idealism from such
ravages. Why not, under a sway so profoundly
gentle as this, give the act a credence that, in
other light, seemed to demand disapprobriation, the
account of which, at odd measures, might even be

taken if the alarm first not sounds that, painstakingly
no more the proviso than encampment, only to force full
well the recondite consideration that what is by such
confrontation supposed to later allow is just
what by deference, accommodation to vitiate, would
be then available? Adventure film with poison arrows,
seated in front. By objectifying, that is to say
neutralizing one's regard, allowing the integrity
of the other and all that it cedes by its
dominion. The world deals with negation and
contradiction and does not assert any single
scheme. New signs on the federal building, they say
FEDERAL BUILDING. Or whether you're dreaming or just
thinking to yourself. The isolation, the boredom; the
quiet, the space. Why am I not a soul at rest, at
peace? Already around the corner —— are ——. *But*
it's not pain *but* the fear of pain that is terrifying.
And what price to be so peaceful that nothing
is felt or noticed or perturbs. ANXIETY
IS MORTALITY. Is everything, then, prey to your cannibalizing
search for material? Such visibility suggests radar
patterns, launching pads. "Sketchily clustered even, these
elements gave out that vague pictorial glow which forms
the first appeal of a living 'subject' to the painter's
consciousness, but the glimmer became intense as I
proceeded to further analysis." *They call me* **Mister**
Tibbs. It is the taint of positive value itself in the mythological

structure; to question, that is, all current correspondences
even the most luminous, lusterous. **False.** Today turns
so that I'm trying, only which helps to explain, now
ensconced, as any place has so much fully to; in
any case we're makes more count as to
getting, still it will be good to see what's waiting.
She shirks complexion, resents having had. Vague
feel of it but no recollection. *Ex dulcit figitur omnibus*
plectum semperis delecto, obit relentere moribus dixum.
For I have wintered in the fields of the Hesperus and tasted
of the starling; this, too, unbears my trial. Though
the question is, how can you lose something you never had?
Accumulation of accommodation, inherent entertainment an
muddled portion. *That grown we weep for want of.*
SLUMPS AS IT PUMPS. "I've got my instinct trained
to a rare morsel of respect." That is, that I can see myself.
They produced thick tomato sandwiches, saying with pride
that they were brought from Woolworth's. One screw
missing, but you can air condition us all; some kind of far
away village, behind it. Don't you find it chilly
sitting with your Silly? Yet things
beguile us with their beauty
their sullen irascibility: the hay of the
imagination is the solace of a dry soul; which
is to say, keep yourselves handy since
you may be called on at any hour.
One wants almost to shudder (yawn, laugh . . .) in disbelief

at the hierarchization of consciousness in such a dictum
as "first thought, best thought", as if recovery
were to be prohibited from the kingdom;
for anyway "first thought" is no thinking
at all. There is no 'actual space of'. So
quiet you can hear the clouds gather. Weep
not, want not; but there's such a thing as being
numb. "As if you could kill time without injuring eternity."
I'm screaming at somebody or being screamed at, not
interesting enough to wake up for. Slurps
as it burps. FIRST BURP, BEST BURP. "You take it very well,"
he says admiringly. "I don't think I would have been as
cheerful if Uncle Bill hadn't given me money." The
Case of the Missing Coagulate. *Emphysema* / Nice to see ya.
'Some such succor' 'monozite don't treat
me right' 'infestation of prognostication'.
"You have such a horrible sense of equity which
is inequitable because there's no such
things as equity." *The text, the beloved?*
Can I stop living when the pain gets too
great? Nothing interrupts this moment.
False.

THE VOYAGE OF LIFE

Over the remote hills, which seem
to intercept the stream, and turn
in from its hitherto direct
course, a path is dimly seen, tending
directly toward that cloudy Fabric
which is the object and desire
of the Voyager. —THOMAS COLE

Resistance marries faith, not faith persist-
Ence. Which is to say, little to import
Or little brewed from told and anxious
Ground: an alternating round of this or
That, some outline that strikes the looking back,
That gives the Punch and Judy to our show.
If it be temperate, it is temper-
Ance that make us hard; by strength of purpose
Turn Pinocchio into ox or gore
Melons with pickaxes, which the fighting
Back in turn proposes slugged advantage,
Slumped discomfit: rashes of ash, as
On a scape to ripple industry with
Hurls, the helter finds in shrubbing stuns. We
Carve and so are carved in twofold swiftness
Of manifold: the simple act of speak-

Ing, having heard, of crossing, having creased.
Sow not, lest reap, and choke on blooming things:
Innovation is Satan's toy, a train
That rails to semblance, place of memory's
Loss. Or tossed in tune, emboss with gloss in-
Signias of air.

THE YEARS AS SWATCHES

Voice seems

to break

over these

short lines

cracking or

setting loose.

I see a word

& it repeats

itself as

your location

overt becalm

that neither

binds nor furnishes:

articles of

cancelled

port

in which I

see you

&

changed by the

mood

return to

sight of

our encounter.

My heart

cleaves

in twos

always

to this

promise

that we

had known but

have forgotten

along the way.

Maze of chaliced

gleam a

menace in

the eyes

clearing

once again.

Gravity's loss:

weight of

hazard's probity

remaindered

on the lawn's

intransigent

green.

Funds deplete

the deeper

fund within

us lode no

one has

found.

And yet

as if, when all—

should current

flood its

days

& self

renounce

in concomitant

polity.

DYSRAPHISM

Did a wind come just as you got up or were
you protecting me from it? I felt the abridgement
of imperatives, the wave of detours, the saber-
rattling of inversion. *All lit up and no*
place to go. Blinded by avenue and filled with
adjacency. Arch or arched at. So there becomes bottles,
hushed conductors, illustrated proclivities for puffed-
up benchmarks. Morose or comatose. "Life is what
you find, existence is what you repudiate." A good example
of this is 'Dad pins puck.' Sometimes something
sunders; in most cases, this is no more than a hall.
No where to go but pianissimo (protection of market
soaring). "Ma always fixes it just like I
like it." Or here valorize what seem to put off
in other. No excuse for that! You can't
watch ice sports with the lights on! Abnormal fluid retention,
inveterate inundation. Surely as wrongheaded as
but without its charm. No identification, only
restitution. But he has forced us to compel this offer;
it comes from policy not love. "Fill
the water glasses—ask each person
if they would like
more coffee, etc." *Content's*
dream. The
journey is

far, the

rewards inconsequential. Heraldically defamed.

Go—it's—gotten. Best

of the spoils: gargoyles. Or is a pretend wish

that hits the springs to sing with sanguine

bulk. "Clean everything from the table except

water, wine, and ashtrays; use separate plate to

remove salt & pepper." Ignorant

I confront, wondering at

I stand. We need

to mention that this is one

that applies to all eyes and that its application is only on the

most basic and rudimentary

level. Being

comfortable with and also

inviting and satisfying.

The pillar's tale: a windowbox onto society.

But heed not the pear that blows in your

brain. God's poison is the concept of

conceptlessness—anaerobic breath.

No less is culled no more vacated—temptation's

flight is always to

beacon's hill—the soul's

mineshaft.

Endless strummer. There is never annul-

ment, only abridgment. The Northern Lights is

the universe's paneled basement. Joy

when jogged. Delight in

forefright. Brushstrokes
on the canals of the . . . , moles on
sackcloth. "People like you don't need
money—you breed contempt." Some way such
toxic oases. This growth of earls, as on a failing
day, gurgling arboreally. Shoes that
shock. I'd
give to you my monkey, my serenade, my shopping bag;
but you require constancy, not weights. Who
taking the lump denies the pot, a beam of
buckram. Or they
with their, you
with your. Another
shot, another stop—dead
as floor board. Pardon my declension: short
parade. "Refill platter and pass to
everybody." A
sound is a sum—a sash
of seraphs. Bored loom.
Extension is never more than a form of content. "I
know how you feel, Joe. Nobody likes to admit
his girl is that smart." "I feel how you know,
Joe, like nobody to smart that girl is his admit."
A wavering kind of sort—down the tube, doused
in tub, a run of the stairs. You should shoot! But
by the time I'd sided. Magisterially calm and pompous.
Pump ass! A wash

of worry (the worldhood of
the whirl). Or: "Nice being here with anybody." Slips
find the most indefatigable invaginations, surreptitious
requiems.
Surfeit, sure fight.
Otherwise—flies,
detergent whines, flimflam psychosis. Let's:
partition the petulance, roast
the arrears, succor the sacred. "If you don't keep up
with culture, culture will keep up
with you." Sacral dosing, somewhat
hosting. Thread
threads the threads, like
thrush. Thrombolytic cassette. "While all of this is
going on, young Sir Francis Rose—a painter of dubious
gifts whom Gertrude Stein espoused for the last decade
of her life—appears as if out of nowhere with a
painting." If you mix with him you're mixing
with a metaphor. "It's
a realistic package, it's a
negotiable package, it's
not a final package." Glibness
of the overall, maybe: there is always something dripping
through.
We seem to be retreading the same tire
over and over, with no additional traction. Here
are some additional panes—optional. Very busy

by now reorganizing and actually, oddly, added
into fractionation ratio, as you might say. Or just
hitting against, back to everybody.
Reality is always greener
when you haven't seen her.
Anyway just to go on and be where you weren't or couldn't be
before—steps, windows, ramps. To let
all that other not so much dissolve as
blend into an horizon of distraction, distension
pursued as homing ground
(a place to bar the leaks). Say,
vaccination of cobalt emissaries pregnant with bivalent
exasperation, protruding with inert material. I
can't but sway, hopeful in my way. Perhaps
portend, tarry. The galoshes are, e.g.,
gone; but you are here. Transient cathexis, Doppler
angst. And then a light comes on
in everybody's head. "So I think
that somewhere we ought to make the point that it's really
a team approach." Riddled
with riot. What
knows not scansion admits
expansion: tea leaves
decoy
for the grosser fortune—the slush
of afternoon, the morning's replay. Prose,
pose—relentless

furrier.

Poem, chrome. "I
don't like the way you think":
a mind is a terrible thing to spend.
That is, in prose you start with the world
and find the words to match; in poetry you start
with the words and find the world in them. "Bring
soup in—very hot." "You
couldn't find your way
out of a blanched potato." Silence
can also be a tool
but it is seldom as effective as blindness.
His quarter, and heir to his heart, whom he purpled
with his fife, does bridle purpose to pursue
tides with unfolded scowls, and, pinched in this
array, fools compare with slack-weary ton.
Dominion demands distraction—the circus
ponies of the slaughter home. Braced
by harmony, bludgeoned by decoration
the dream surgeon hobbles three steps over, two
steps beside. "In those days you didn't have to
shout to come off as expressive." One by one
the clay feet are sanded, the sorrows remanded.
A fleet of ferries, forever merry.
Show folks know that what the fighting man wants
is to win the war and come home.

AMBLYOPIA

He was a moral dwarf in a body as
solid as ice. Everywhere he looked
he felt fear and
evasion. No notice
no location bore any
resemblance to the true
form of these cinders:
intransigence, pestering. It
was the logic of
insurgence, a stone door
opening onto a dirt
floor. For three weeks
he stayed there, only 50
feet from the geyser
watching his footsteps
rattle. From time to
time, he rolled up the floor
and looked to the expanse
below. The physical
present, he would say
to himself, is unrelated to the
physical afterthought. Towns
steamed in the
light: a glimmer

of the ghosts of the people who had
lived there.

Personality is barbarity
so we eat at each other
with waxing spirits when
all the time we are on the
wane. No stop exists
except what we manufacture
the need for. The Heart
is a steel brace that men
use to erect their sagging spirits.
I am not I because my
sister has stolen a
pear and I have tasted of
its pit. The light
was (is) stuck. Mourners gnaw
at the columns.

Allegorical micturition has swept
the guest halls of the art galleries
and the undermasses
wail in the background to iambic
beat. Sludge is proclaimed sludge,
hairdos hors d'oeuvres, as the soiled
face of inverted cardioerasty—a.k.a.
genital fetish—rears its mushy brow.

The excellence of our gifts humbles
us into cleverness when before we were
only foolish. *Blessed are the grieved* for
they at least have seen their
inheritance; the rest wait in maxivans
to collect as available. THE BITTER COKE
OF JIMMY CARTER; the greased palm, the
adored swan; all are crepuscular,
dilated, dogged, dictated. For others,
orgasm is achieved only by means
of words without any tactile contact;
some married women report depraved
husbands who force them to submit
to this practice. "It may be cheap
but it's not worth that much."

From the Ministry of Psychological Science:
Normal minds never run adrift when there are no environmental
factors to poison them. Exposure to big businessmen, right-to-life
Christians, military officers, career managers, and *New York Times*
cultural editors causes otherwise healthy young people to become
perverts. These types, motivated by greed for money and power and
authority belong to the lower human strata. They are classed as
moral imbeciles. They are all, or most of them, antisocials with a pro-
nounced defective aesthetic sense. It is not uncommon, however, to
find them brilliant and nimble witted. But they are plausible and
ready liars. They lie even when the truth might be more serviceable.

Lifestyles that would arouse horror and repugnance in normal persons are sought after by such individuals. People of this type resent being spoken to courteously; they want to be addressed roughly. Even among those classed as intelligent, they derive actual gratification in exposing their ignorance to one another. Many have anesthetic consciences—pricks with needles cause no pain. Orgasms can only be achieved by this type of pervert by enacting or fantasizing racist, sexist, ageist, or authoritarian acts. Having once been an unwilling witness to conversation between two such individuals, I can say it is the most disgusting, absolutely the most nauseating, spectacle one can imagine.

Solitude and contentment are the product
of the mystical; we are never
alone and, by rights, never at peace.
Such is a space that, called
into being, or given,
transforms everything from what we
know it to be, mishandled by
the world, to what it never was, blessed.
(Or handled: but since there is
no correct way to handle, it amounts
continuously to the same.) A bed of
smoke and pearls—tripped by
the sum, troped by the tune. No
cordon ever warms the soul, but
a simple costless gesture may. Yet

the act is not made but found, nor
yet discovered—nothing hides.

So begins the long march to the
next world. Custom is abandoned
outright as a criterion of moral
conduct. Everything must be justified
before the courts of the New Criteria, which
spring out of the old with the resourcefulness
and tenacity of the truly ingrained. The theory
of primary colors is rejected as elitist
empiricism and the wavelengths of the spectrum
take their proper and equal place in
the constitution of perception. Garrulousness
is taken for honesty.

Related to this—the excitement, the dancing
around, articulating itself in terms of these,
& getting, this might, the sanctioned
"drive and concentration", more
obviously through—dinner, TV—
in some sense entertained ("I tried
all kinds of things")—"open
ended" "divergent level"—as to
rehearsal, to assume the spirit of,
balanced against, practically

speaking, an unresolvable fend.
As harmful regardless, at which
at in was assessment, without
circumstance to enter, to be found in,
& often strategic almost total compensation,
hallmark comparably, innately
literally, operate by, overstatement,
endorsement, restriction, as if it
was already having our, as the
most, she or he along, suspect
that, that which, putting aside,
as such, cadres of the (steaming,
identification, insofar) in which
segmenting, say to stay,
technologically gathered, etc.,
into mass utter anomaly with,
if you hold, "get ahead" hot
bed, fosters as being outside
one is "alertness" or for
tapped, assigned, passed over,
inverted. A highly visible necessary,
& those is a safety valve to as
usual, designated but saved from the
meantime, would present, there is also,
apart from these, regarding are
largely.

The tubs rectify obliquely whatever
they decant, but this is not a
guarantee of much more than ingestion.
Whether there is a forge or a
spill, such that what is
represented is regarded with
spears, or does alarm come along
like, what's the vision and what
the version, a bland potentate
of flak. These are
ordinary triads. Why not recover
the innuendo of stultification
the grey gloat of glory?
For instance, hopping a pail, chewing
a nail, while all along a bone
spoke in the crag. Gushes of
static cling. It is not the eye
but it's gleam of which we dream.

This is my suffice to a world of
toast, "which so raptures the
spirits, delights the gust, and gives
such airs to the countenance as are
not to be imagined by those who
have not tried it". Apostate
rings girded by avalanche.
Whose history demands

carbon, which insinuate
formaldehyde. Discipline demands
not looking back, depotentiate dirigible
doorjambs, districted lapilli
thus extended: sworn fuss, brazen
discretion.

Shuns (shuts) tourmaline—indigestion
apparently apocrypha, red line.
Beeline to inadequacy, repossess pose
(by posse?). Integration of burn at distal
curve: go, gum, go. Govern get
away, resettlement crematoria, dog's
duty, prioritate. What's in it for (John's
Hancock)? Oblique cartel, gummed up
gust. Free clogging restored, myst-
ified. The harmony of harangue (dodeca
do(dad, mom)). With all the passion of
a plum, bowl of milk. Ha! see end
of (adobe).

INFORMATION ABOUT THE RATE ON PURCHASE
AND THE BALANCE
BY WHICH EACH IS JUDGED. The
Balance of every Purchase is an average
Daily Balance. Each daily Purchase
is added in the Life Cycle for, as

applicable, Purchase incurred before
the Conversion Date and Purchase incurred
on or after the Conversion Date. Each
day is begun with the opening Balance
for the Life Cycle for whatever Purchase
and all new Purchase and other
debts are added (including any posted
that day), subtracting all Payment and other
Credits posted to the Principal since the start
of the Life Cycle (including any posted
that day). The Daily Balance for Purchase
incurred on or after the Conversion Date
is as follows: each day is
begun with the opening Balance for the
Life Cycle for Purchase and all New Purchase
and other debts posted to the Principal
since the start of the Life Cycle (including
any posted that day), subtracting as before
(including any posted that day). However
there is no Balance for
Purchase incurred either before or on
or after the Conversion Date in any
Life Cycle in which there is no
Previous Balance for Purchase, or in which all
Payments and other Credits applied to Purchase
for the Life Cycle at least equal the

Previous Balance for all Purchase for the
Life Cycle.

Thus will these hovers goad, the lurk's
amount to saddle its detour, relinquishing
two snares and a brandy-colored
drain, inside themselves, and six
pace on, to halt at precipice. No
peace abjures like the bleat of desalinated
tears, with which to wash tomorrow's
coarse inveigh. Consider stance a
suck upon portent's languid sneer.

The world grows simpler, or I
ajangle in its pores—so
simple one might dote upon
refrains or balk at balm.
"No other vision exists except
the single crane—they call it
tracking—on a green-brown
backing."

Neither for what or without—

An incredible growling hush besets, or
sets over, this pall of purpose. Testing

the certitude of fortitude, the quiescence
of restitution. Everything as it always
was, or will (would) want to be—
ferreting a cataract from a sublime
act, the knees and pancreas of boisterous
dispose. Mildness and omitted
emotions.

Everything external to turn
of the last out of accumulated, dig
slowly, piles trying about, which were
flaw, fugitive, indeed lights, but when
mind of stumbles that on accurate
has to do which became early, say
at, might just as it is, clash, that
by mainly intentions, subjected
as if, were—officious tone—nickel &
dimed or being any given to do
something that that on our—you
should, that is, to handle—even
come up with what amounts to, for
keeping or setting of respect of lack
literally trying to prolong, complain
apparent, is to rather condescended
correlative as to blind, off, by
attitude.

substitution dubbed

The clothes are clogged, the
blistering revamped, all the pleonasms
gone away. What chord, cowed
lingers as the lurker takes its
nightly flight? Beyond these realms—
ingots made of air; or not-quite
air, that less were substance of a dream.
Or beam remote into exaction
obliterated grace of stubborn hand.

Or in which ornate matter is dispersed
to the sarcophagi of circumstance
or in which, lamented by the swell
torches cascade in fractions of
notions left as
elevated or whether who so may, withstanding
lock, block, & pork—indiscriminate
originarys, reputable gulls, while
wistfully wandering at the end-platform
vouchsafing their—eye will already
spatter in dejectable detonate, re-
furbishment to high cantorial yarn
per yard would be cantankerously
mortuary, which fails, hales—

The new begins again, slips behind—
not more to wish than to redress,
sacrament of superfluity in the (a) realm
of frowns. There is a crimson
counter, an alabaster fountain—on
the other side.

Where do you want to ride? It's
all a matter of dejection & sub-
limation, illusion & collusion.
So called surreal surcease, badger
endeavour to enjoin. Here are heroes, bison
with functioning mindsets, dictaphone
artists, domestic doodlers. The cup-
cake of tranquillity, the earache of—

There is neither matter nor form, only
smell, taste, bite—eyes
hide by their disclosure. There
is only substance—structure—twin
fears of an unduplicating repetition:
the sandstorm of grief, the presentlessness
of distribution. As farfetched
ministers to its own resolve
purpose alone is the proprietor
of the poignant, vesture of solace's
lazy haze.

Keep a curb on your brain. The heart
beats thrice where the soul has lost
its foot. The campground of larceny
is the foremast of destination's deprecation.
Still, no teleology holds here. Gather
what rims you may, hold tight to
clandestine animation, besalt aggravation.
Out of a pure sludge . . . and to sludge
shall you—remain.

The heir of circumstance, the in of
inarticulation. Stepping off a
train, a station liner, a moth
ball. Floating into incandescent frostbite.
How these avenues arise in arrears.
Joining our Savior, boring our way
here. I've got—why not get—
strip cash, milk of

"He's made an art of not remembering."

The pierced fluidity of a smile that
battles reportorial mink stoles, solvent
greasers in gumptious dodecahedrons.
Why wet these belts, revamp
a tire? Milkmaid of respect, jilted
of dismay. Go, get, gone—

"Perception does not merely serve
to confirm preexisting assumptions, but
to provide orgasms with new
information." Standing around the
kitchen, talking 'bout boats.

A tool of philosophy.

Who (which) garner anyway, any-
where (why). Panes fly dirigibles, or
foment surface shimmer (chimera). Beige
lofts the two of us (whether) signalling
retreat—enhance—repeat—entrance. Slow
beat the bugles on Murray's soured
block—clappity clap, jiffity jig. There
is no refusal that outlives
handprints, suction weight. Thence
thwart a (of) formica biscuit cut-
ter, all through the seas. A clue 'ugs
butter—(vats)—

Many people have trouble with everyday
activities, such as speaking, thinking,
responding, dreaming, eating, sleeping. A crutch
shares the weight of burden, protecting
without shielding, but should not be used
without specific instructions.

Untoward by—these detach with
salmon or scrubmate severance
not anywhere detained by
oaken chair, wavering as the wind
whirls around Brenda Starr, eschatological
venison. I abide by later
egging, tomahawk remonstration.
Or is this gulled, posted, and
foreshortened? Who activates
you biscuit us insets, um,
er, insects. Colonies of spears,
a minority of heres.

cares caned

Whoever therefore blemishes into
interlock—defamed retainer, absorbent
factotum. Which wish reserves
armoire. Here he lunges (interpeptide
nudge) at workmanlike manure, sharp
presser. Ache of the pancreas, fate
of the polyurethaned didact. Emblemized
by tries.

The flip side of organdy—still
lace face, fretted surprise, "Jam"
Whistler. An or am emendation of

beside all preemptive repair. Gliding
in indigo boxcars, hiding in
viewmaster canister. Golan Heights
swollen price.

No scheme completes the falling down
of chairs, of cards, or igloos
sprayed in camel dust. The motion
spares the inbred count, where
clumps at curious coventry steam
seas of sailors' sorrows.

From this adoration unrolls more smoke—
eyed voyeurs with whooping
coughs. Those afterward, strolling
out of their lofts and heliotropes
displacing memorized variety
with hallucinogenic contempt, lather
up their secretions and spew them
at— Convicted of charm
conspicuous with greed.

And Now . . .
JUST WHEN YOU THOUGHT IT WAS TIME
TO STOP THINKING AGAIN . . .
Texton introduces the Whipmaster Valorizer™
Yes . . .

Just when you thought you were stuck in the same
old shopworn anxieties and tired-out guilt
feelings, the Whipmaster Valorizer™ has arrived,
revolutionizing the psychopoetics industry.
In just seconds, you can turn your sordid dreams
and ambitions into cherished *res intellectiones*.
The Valorizer uses a unique Twofold action.
Negative associations are effaced from habitual
cognitions by a sanitized derealization process.
Simultaneously, positive associations are affixed
to these cognitions by means of thousands of tiny
Idealization Crystals®, a unique adhesion agent.
The Whipmaster Valorizer™ is available exclusively
from Texton, your better living through alchemistry
company.

"What is this, a marathon?" Strolling in
admonition, bowling in derivation. Weave our
way in mordant display. For a day
is not a dome, nor an estuary a
delegation. Reminiscent of restitution, perennial
towel-master, tuck-a-way bonfire, cloaks
the longing for lard (largesse). Museum of
double blinds: clubbable behind, whereless weathers.

Locations lock the far side of.
Not that riddles, little by little a

momento of seed; oasis of reproach
gusts the beatitudes tiny stare, lording
it over sword sway. Imperial
allure at ground zero. Forget,
forfeit. The journey is stern
benefactor to the departing caboose.
Ride the querulous hound.

FROM *FOREIGN BODY SENSATION*

"I am especially interested in the treatment of depression. With my Lord and Savior Jesus Christ at the center of my life, I have found real Joy and Purpose in dedicating myself to the Truth of His Teaching as Written in the Bible. What gives the job its excitement is working with Stan Richards, a nationally recognized creative wizard: *Adweek* recently named our agency among the eight most creative in the U.S. I moved into this area after six years in the aerospace industry, which I entered after early retirement from a career as a venture capitalist and real estate developer. This has been a stimulating opportunity for my work on late Pleistocene and early Holocene environmental changes. Pat is currently in Sri Lanka helping organize sera collection for leprosy patients. Nowadays, being a husband, father, homeowner, and Jew keeps me both busy and satisfied. I find myself immersed in a foreign but also satisfyingly tangible world of container shipping. I still find the labor movement to be the (imperfect) representative of workers' interests, and the necessary base from which the realization of class structure in economic and social life is explained and organized into coherent, worker-oriented politics. It wasn't long before I found myself in the company of a spiritual adept who teaches the most profound way of transcendence of every kind of self-possession. Left the firm and freelanced in stained glass. I studied hula seriously in Hawaii and taught Hawaiian dance locally, forming a group to hire out for bar mitzvahs and luaus. To my knowledge this is a unique occurrence, of great spiritual and cultural significance. My work has taken me into the area of robotics and industrial automation. For several years I worked in insurance, specializing in kidnap and expropriation coverage. A professional interest has been in the area of domestic violence; I love the work and feel strongly about violent crime. For a while, I served in the Peace Corps in Guatemala as a nurse working with cancer patients. After two years in Met State, I became increasingly eager to work with severely disturbed children. I am beginning to dabble in writing screenplays, humor, and poetry. What time is left I devote to coursework at the Divinity School, where I am studying for the priesthood. It seems I have done other things also, but maybe not. I guess I. In the future, I look forward to the private practice of pathology. Just when that will occur is uncertain. I am now administering substances to others to alter or obliterate their consciousness. The break is wonderful. Though nothing has educated me as well as watching my father walk the picket line in a strike that was eventually broken."

"Come, Shadow, Come"

    return to a shadow
as slope of mind,
         veiled air,
      (the way a thought will turn
             with a gesture in its direction—
        you are a thing
   your voices are unreal
        blade, pool,
           paper, shavings

        its glassiness waving for us

THE HARBOR OF ILLUSION

At midnight's scrawl, the fog has
lost its bone and puffs of
pall are loamed at
tidal edge. No more to count
than density arrows its
petulance at crevice laced
with dock, not hour's
solstice nor brimmed detour—
over the haunch of lock and
tress the vein pours sweetly
and Devil's door knows no
more than pester and undone—
the seering moors where I
refrain of lot and camphor.
Only this, a ripple
against a blind of shore that sands
us smooth and mistless: let
he who has not stunned make
sound, cacophany of
nearing, having fell, of
pouring, having stalled. Though
free to bore and load, let
rail retail conclusion, finicky jejubes
at waste of moor, or lord these
tower, tour the template, thoroughfare
of noon's atoll.

AUTONOMY IS JEOPARDY

I hate artifice. All these
contraptions so many barriers
against what otherwise can't
be contested, so much seeming
sameness in a jello of
squirms. Poetry scares me. I
mean its virtual (or ventriloquized)
anonymity—no protection, no
bulwark to accompany its pervasive
purposivelessness, its accretive
acceleration into what may or
may not swell. Eyes demand
counting, the nowhere seen everywhere
behaved voicelessness everyone is clawing
to get a piece of. Shudder
all you want it won't
make it come any faster
last any longer: the pump
that cannot be dumped.

THE KIWI BIRD IN THE KIWI TREE

I want no paradise only to be
drenched in the downpour of words, fecund
with tropicality. Fundament be-
yond relation, less 'real' than made, as arms
surround a baby's gurgling: encir-
cling mesh pronounces its promise (not bars
that pinion, notes that ply). The tailor tells
of other tolls, the seam that binds, the trim,
the waste. & having spelled these names, move on
to toys or talcums, skates & scores. Only
the imaginary is real—not trumps
beclouding the mind's acrobatic vers-
ions. The first fact is the social body,
one from another, nor needs no other.

Who's on first? The dust descends as
the skylight caves in. The door
closes on a dream of default and
denunciation (go get those piazzas),
hankering after frozen (prose) ambiance
(ambivalence). Doors to fall in, bells
to dust, nuances to circumscribe.
Only the real is real: the little
girl who cries out "Baby! Baby!"
but forgets to look in the mirror
—of a . . . It doesn't really
matter whose, only the appointment
of a skewed and derelict parade.
My face turns to glass, at last.

VERDI AND POSTMODERNISM

She walks in beauty like the swans
that on a summer day do swarm
& crawls as deftly as a spoon
& spills & sprawls & booms.

These moments make a monument
then fall upon a broken calm
they fly into more quenchless rages
than Louis Quatorze or Napoleon.

If I could make one wish I might
overturn a state, destroy a kite
but with no wishes still I gripe
complaint's a Godly-given right.

RIDDLE OF THE FAT FACED MAN

None guards the moor where stands
Receipt of scorn, doting on doddered
Mill as fool compose compare, come
Fair padre to your pleated score
Mind the ducks but not the door
Autumnal blooms have made us snore

OF TIME AND THE LINE

George Burns likes to insist that he always
takes the straight lines; the cigar in his mouth
is a way of leaving space between the
lines for a laugh. He weaves lines together
by means of a picaresque narrative;
not so Henny Youngman, whose lines are strict-
ly paratactic. My father pushed a
line of ladies' dresses—not down the street
in a pushcart but upstairs in a fact'ry
office. My mother has been more concerned
with her hemline. Chairman Mao put forward
Maoist lines, but that's been abandoned (most-
ly) for the East-West line of malarkey
so popular in these parts. The prestige
of the iambic line has recently
suffered decline, since it's no longer so
clear who "I" am, much less who *you* are. When
making a line, better be double sure
what you're lining in & what you're lining
out & which side of the line you're on; the
world is made up so (Adam didn't so much
name as delineate). Every poem's got
a prosodic lining, some of which will
unzip for summer wear. The lines of an

imaginary are inscribed on the
social flesh by the knifepoint of history.
Nowadays, you can often spot a work
of poetry by whether it's in lines
or no; if it's in prose, there's a good chance
it's a poem. While there is no lesson in
the line more useful than that of the pick-
et line, the line that has caused the most ad-
versity is the bloodline. In Russia
everyone is worried about long lines;
back in the USA, it's strictly soup-
lines. "Take a chisel to write," but for an
actor a line's got to be cued. Or, as
they say in math, it takes two lines to make
an angle but only one lime to make
a Margarita.

THE LIVES OF THE TOLL TAKERS

There appears to be a receiver off the hook. Not that

you care.

      Beside the gloves resided a hat and two

pinky rings, for which no

finger was ever found. Largesse

      with no release became, after

not too long, atrophied, incendiary,

           stupefying. Difference or

différance: it's

the distinction between hauling junk and

removing rubbish, while

I, needless not to say, take

out the garbage

(pragmatism)

.

Phone again, phone again jiggity jig.

I figured

they do good eggs here.

Funny $: making a killing on

junk bonds and living to peddle the tale

(victimless rime)

.

(Laughing all the way to the Swiss bank where I put my money
in gold bars
    [the prison house of language]
            .) Simplicity is not

the

same as simplistic.

Sullen

supposition, salacious conjecture, slurpy ded

uction.

"A picture

[fixture]

is worth more than a thousand words":

With this

sally, likely to barely make it

into a 1965 "short stabs" poem

by Ted "bowl over" Berrigan

[*a tincture gives birth to a gravelly verve*]

Barbara Kruger is enshrined in the window

of the Whitney's 1987 Biennial

[*a mixture is worth a thousand one-line serves*].

Nei

ther

speaking the unspeakable nor saying

the
unsayable

(though no doubt slurring

the unslurrable): never only

dedef

ining, always rec

onstricting (libidinal

flow just another

word for loose

st

ools). There was an old lady who lived in a

zoo,

she had so many admirers

she didn't know what to rue. Li

ke

a dull blade with a greasy handle (a

docent page with an

unfathomable ramble). Poetry's

like a spoon, with three or four

exemptions: in effect only

off-peak, void

where permitted by Lord,

triple play

on all designated *ghost* phonemes

(you mean morphemes)
[don't tell me what I mean!
].

   Rhymes may come and

rhymes may go, but ther

      e's

            no crime like presentiment. To refuse

                  the

   affirmation

                  of

(a)

                        straight-forward

      statement

         (sentiment)

                  is

not

to

be

so

bent-over

with

irony

as

to

be

unable

to

assert

anything

but
to
find

such

statement

already

undermined

by the resistance

it

pretends

to

overpower

by

its

idealism

masked as

realism.

What? No approach

too gross if it gets a laugh. In Reagan's

vocabulary, freedom's

just another word for "watch out!" (I

pride myself on my pleonastic a[r]mour.)   {ardour}

(Besides.)

Love may come and love may

go

but uncertainty is here forever.
  {profit?}

(There was an old lady

who lives in a stew . . .)

(A picture is worth 44.95 but no price can be
put on words.)

She can slip and she can slide, she's every

parent's j

        oy & j

    i

       b

 e

    (guide)

      .

In dreams begin a lot of bad
poetry.

Then where is my place?

Fatal Error F27: Disk directory full.

The things I

write are

not about me

though they

become me.

You look so bec

oming, she said, attending the flower pots.

I'm a very

becom

ing guy

(tell it to

)

. That is, better

to

become than
(gestalt f[r]iction)

{traction?}
{flirtation?}

to

be: ac

tuality

is just around

the corner (just a spark

in the dark); self-actualization a glance in

a tank of concave [concatenating] mirrors. Not

angles, just

tangles. From which

a direction emerges, p

urges. Hope

gives way

to tire tracks. On the

way without stipulating

the destination,

the better

to get there (somewhere,

other

).

THE MAGIC PHONEME FOR TODAY IS "KTH".

Funny, you don't look

gluish. Poetry: the show-

me business.

You've just said the magic phoneme!

"Don't give me

any of your

show-me business."

She wore blue velvet but I was color blind and insensible.

Heavy tolls, few

advances. Are you cl

os

e

to your m

other?

The brain of Bill Casey preserved in a glass jar deep under-
cover in Brunei.

Andy

Warhol is the

P. T. Barnum

of the
(late)
twentieth century

:

there's a

succor dead every twenty seconds.

A depository of suppositories

(give it me where it counts:

one and

two and

one

two

thr

eee)

.

I had

it but

I misp

laced

it somewhere

in the

back burner

of what

is laug

hingly

called m

y

mind

(my

crim

e). A

mind is a terrible thing to steal:

   intellectual property is also

   theft.

Ollie North, pound of chalk—but who is writing,

what is writing? Nor

all your regret change one word of it; yet so long as the blood

flows in your veins there is ink

left in the bottle. FAKE A

WHISTLE TO WRITE (*spiritus sancti*). No "mere" readers only

writers who read, actors who inter-

act. Every day fades way, nor

all your piety

or greed bring back one hour: *take a swivel to*

strike.

(The near-heroic obstinacy of his refusal [inability?] to despair.)

    & who

      can say

   whether dejection or elation will

ensure the care for, care

    in

   the world that may lead us

weightless, into a new world or

    sink us, like lead

baboons,

    deeper into this o

       ne? Yet

    you have to admit it's highly

drinkable.

Delish.

I imagine you unbespectacled, upright,

dictating with no hint of undercurrent,

a victim of the tide.

What if

success scares you so much that at the point of some

modest acceptance, midway through

life's burning, you blast out

onto the street, six-shooters smoking, still a rebel.

For what?

Of course new ventures always require risk, but by carefully

analyzing the situation, we became smart risk

takers. Fear of

softness characterized as rounded edges, indecisiveness, need to please

versus the humorless rigidity of the "phallic"

edge, ready

to stand erect, take

sides (false dichotomy, all dichotomies).

An affirmation that dissolves into the fabric of

unaccounted

desires, undertows of an imaginary that cannot be willed away but

neither need be mindlessly

obeyed. *What's that?* If it's not

good news

I don't want to hear it (

stand up and leer.) Our new

service orientation

mea

nt

not only changing the way we wrote poems but also diversifying

into new poetry services. Poetic

opportunities

,

however, do not fall into your lap, at least not

very often. You've got to seek them out, and when you find them

you've got to have the knowhow to take advantage

of them.

Keeping up with the new aesthetic environment is an ongoing

process: you can't stand still. Besides, our current fees

barely cover our expenses; any deviation from these levels

would

mean working for nothing. Poetry services provide cost savings

to readers, such

as avoiding hospitalizations (you're less likely

to get in an accident if you're home reading poems), minimizing

wasted time (*condensare*), and reducing

adverse idea interactions

(studies show higher levels of resistance to double-bind
political programming among those who read 7.7 poems or
more each week

).

Poets deserve compensation

for such services.

For readers unwilling to pay the price

we need to refuse to provide such

services as alliteration,
        internal rhymes,

exogamic structure, and

unusual vocabulary.

Sharp edges which become shady groves,

mosaic walkways, emphatic asymptotes (asthmatic microtolls).

The hidden language of the Jews: self-reproach, laden with
ambivalence, not this or this either, seeing five sides to
every issue, the old *pilpul* song and dance, obfuscation
clowning as ingratiation, whose only motivation is never
offend, criticize only with a discountable barb: Genocide
is made of words like these, Pound laughing (with Nietzsche's
gay laughter) all the way to the canon's bank spewing forth
about the concrete value of gold, the "plain sense of the
word", a people rooted in the land they sow, and cashing
in on such verbal usury (language held hostage: year one
thousand nine hundred eighty seven).

There is no plain sense of the word,

nothing is straightforward,

description a lie behind a lie:

but truths can still be told.

These are the sounds of science (whoosh, blat,
flipahineyhoo), brought to
you by DuPont, a broadly diversified company dedicated to
exploitation through science and industry.

Take this harrow off

my chest, I don't feel it anymore

it's getting stark, too stark

to see, feel I'm barking at Hell's spores.

The new sentience.

As if Harvard Law School

was not a re-education camp.

I had decided to go back

to school after fifteen years in

community poetry because I felt

I did not know enough to navigate

through the rocky waters that

lie ahead for all of us in this field.

How had Homer done it, what might Milton

teach? Business training turned

out to be just what I most needed.

Most importantly, I learned that

for a business to be successful, it

needs to be different, to stand out

from the competition. In poetry,

this differentiation is best

achieved through the kind of form

we present.

Seduced by its own critique, the heady operative with twin
peaks and a nose for a brain, remodeled the envelope she

was pushing only to find there was nobody home and no time when they were expected. Water in the brain, telescopic Malthusian dumbwaiter, what time will the train arrive?, I feel weird but then I'm on assignment, a plain blue wrapper with the taps torn, sultan of my erogenous bull's eyes, nothing gratis except the tall tales of the Mughali terraces, decked like plates into the Orangerie's glacial presentiment . . .

No,

only that the distinction

between nature and

culture may obs

cure

the

b
odily

gumption of language.

Hello

my name is Max Gomez

(g

houlis

hness is it

s own rewa

rd).

(Commanding without being a command.)

Or else to say,

Catalogs are free, why not we?

Clear as f

udge.

Then what can I believe in?

(She'd rather exploit

than be exploi

ted.) If you break it, you

won't have it anymore.

Solemn in functional midrift, tooting at

bellicose grinding, who can no more bear witness to the doddering

demise of diplomacy than uproot the cancer at the throat of those

trajectories.

"Daddy, what did you

do to stop the war?"

[p-
=]ovwhiu2g97hgbcf67q6dvqujx67sf21g97b.c.9327b97b987b87b87j 7
7td7tq98gdukbhq g9tq9798 icxqyj2f108ytscxags62jc   . <Mz[
-\ io

We may be all one body but we're sure as hell not one mind.

(Tell her I had to

change my plans.) It's not

what you

know but

who knows

about it

& who's

likely to

                                        squeal

      .   *Button*

your lip, cl

    asp your tie, you

  ,

    re on the B team. (A job

  by any other name

would smell as

  sour.) *It's*

not an operating system it

,

s an

op

erating environm

ent.

Besides

VIRTUAL REALITY

FOR SUSAN

Swear
   there is a sombrero
of illicit
      desquamation
(composition).

         I forgot to
   get the
         potatoes but the lakehouse
   (ladle)
      is spent
   asunder. Gorgeous
         gullibility—
or,
      the origin
      of testiness
   (testimony).

Laura
   does the laundry, Larry
lifts lacunas.

Such that
details commission of
        misjudgment over 30-day
intervals.

                By
the sleeve is the
        cuff & cuff
link (lullaby, left offensive,
        houseboat).
Nor
        let your unconscious
get the better of you.
        Still, all ropes
lead somewhere, all falls
        cut to fade.
I.e.: 4 should always be followed
        by 6, 6 by 13.

    Or if
        individuality is a false
front, group solidarity is a
    false fort.

"ANY MORE FUSSING & YOU'LL
        GO RIGHT TO YOUR ROOM!"

She flutes that slurp
admiringlier.

Any more blustering & I
collapse as deciduous
replenishment.

So sway the
swivels, corpusculate the
dilatations.
For I've
learned that relations
are a small
twig in the blizzard
of projections
& expectations.
The story
not capacity but care—
not size but desire.

& despair
makes dolts of any persons, shimmering
in the quiescence of
longing, skimming
disappointment & mixing it
with
breeze.

The sting of
recognition triggers
the memory & try to
take that apart (put
that together).

            Popeye
no longer sails, but Betty
      Boop will always
          sing sweetlier
          sweetliest
than the crow who fly
      against the blank
      remorse of castles made
      by dusk, dissolved in
                  day's baked light.

REVEAL CODES

It is often said that the bladder is an unreliable
witness. I've felt that way myself coming back
from a sluggishly encumbered day at the computer
bank. "They clammed up like so many turtles
in overdrive"—but only if you didn't get to know
their Mercurial propulsions. There's a version
that says quell the branches before you braid
or at least unload the interfusing hot buttons. Don't
know much about chopped wax either, loop
the reliquary, some cross-valent comet coming at
50,000 kilobytes per minute per mention, I left
the rack at the store but recalled the combination
to the cross, "he would suck up to
an octopus if he thought it would strangle somebody
for him", no pork barrel just juiced petunias . . .

It was one of those almost unfamiliar
sections of LA, just beyond the tar
pits, where you could get steak
& eggs for breakfast for under ten
& change. I wasn't
quite a regular but they knew me well enough

to bring the order without asking
too many questions. It was
a dive I went to to get my mind off work, my attention
Intermittent Diffuse
with just enough juice
to register the scene at the end table
by the picture of Hydra.

Ripping through the water like it was so much
Swiss cheese

"The only thing Swiss about you is the baloney!"

Dear Mr. Charles,
I wish and pray this letter finds you
in the best of health and cheers. May I
introduce myself as a missionary priest
working for North East India with its
thousands of downtrodden people, suffering
from the pangs of poverty, illiteracy
diseases, etc. Hence in their name this
begging letter to you for any little help.
So many innocent and poor children
are to be fed, educated, and looked
after. Timely aids for emergency needs

give us tensions in distress we
have no other way than to make
appeal in folded hands to kind
hearted people.

Fr. Pallatty M.
Madras 600 008

Dried ice or crunched innuendo, on your toes then on your
knees. To capitalize Despair—that was the old way; to
capitalize on despair, who promises an aspiring future
in piece goods . . . The boat found the hay but the ocean
had turned to a symphony of suction. *So long sweet tuna,*
so long gefilte fish. The only true traditions
the ones we invent to vent the spleen of the inconsolable
loss of history's ambient diffusion and victory's
unsparing parry. Witless in the rain, sober
in the dew . . .

Or more due than ever done, when debts
Soak the morning and regrets eventide

> My name is Necromancer
> My sister calls me Still
> I'm widely known as Cast Away
> 've trouble with my Trill

Yet despite the disintegration of his personality, the
foolishness of his actions, his excessive drunkenness
and incurable extravagance, Goldsmith was, and is,
a great man—a man of rare talents that border on
genius, one of the finest natural writers in the English
language.

For Blake's art is ornamental
& rhetorical, not organic &
formal.

Slip & slide
pop 'n' fizz
blink and whine
drop, spin

There hangs the fade, there the woolen shoes.
The roof has swoops—
two fools under one hood, alarmed to the teeth
one with an eye on the sail
other with ear to the—.

Where the carcass is, there
the crow flies.

Swarming around the bandshell
waiting for the buzz saw

or Buick Pompadour convertible
coupe or any so-called doze-proof
buffet

Or, to put it more bluntly, no gain
no pain. As if no pain wasn't
pain enough.

This buttons the cue when the overlay
is toggled. "Hot keys"—i.e.
combinations you press to access
a resident, or underlying, program, as
"control" and "home", "mother" and "blanket",
"disguise" and "revenge".

As in a lifeguard's better than
no guard. As if
you could guard life
without blanking it out.

My friend Polly Vocal called the other
day just to say hello. I decided not
to pick up and returned the call
to the machine on her other number.

Go On Get Down

"Do they have a bar here?"

Short stabs or quick hits or is there
an exit & is it near the "exit" sign?

Is the Pope Polish? Does 3 + 5 equal 5 + 3?
Is Lincoln buried in Grant's Tomb? Is
the South Bronx a WASP enclave? Will this
burn at Fahrenheit 451? Is Napoleon the President
of the Bahamas? Is Communism finished? Do
hearts break when you don't touch them?
Are the rich getting richer or are you just
glad to see me?

"I didn't give it to you with any sand so
why do you give it to me with sand?"

"Well, Blanche, I just brought the egg over here
because the recipe says to separate two eggs."

LET'S CALL THE POLICE!

"Let's call the Swedish delegation!"

Call me irresistible or call me unreliable
but don't call me I'll call you

He showed a malignant unwillingness to differentiate
frames suggesting an underlying refusal
to distinguish between performative, substantive,
substantive-performative, and perfermo-substantive
utterances.

"I thought utterances were for cows"

"You think you're big but in reality you're
very little"

"In reality" I don't exist though I will recently
have moved to Buffalo.

Elbow or buckled philodendron

"It's just hard it's not like you're gonna get killed"

First there is the build up & then the fizz (fix).
In Utopia the story will never end.

—"Or begin"

"Yah but a softball is still hard"

Or if this followed the other, that this? This that
other, the followed this if, or.

Just don't say it like you mean it

You can't substitute *heating oil* for 'moral panic'

You get the hose, I got the biscuits

Look! Look!

I'm eternally attentive but nowhere sentient

"Just tell the snake, 'NO'!"

Fluidly floral or floridly fluid

Butcha better belch

"No they're not fighting it's real play"

She doesn't give up she doesn't even try!

Flummoxed or flunked or flushed or refrigerator

Decals make the man much the way oilcloth
makes the kitchen. "Oilcloth" being an old-
fashioned way of saying *linoleum*, "decals"
being an oblique way of suggesting *models for*.

"I'm hungry and want someone to greet"

If sand'll get you shore, sad'll get
you exactly nowhere.

"But I can't help it"

"Then I can't help you"

(As if volition were voluntary)

You have to occupy yourself sometimes, draw
on your own resources.

As if *you* had any!

My inner resources are overdrawn, in the
sense of interest due *&* exaggerated, which go
together like an ant and a pineapple,
a zebra and polystyrene wrap, petunia
and DOS 4.01.

DOS, DOS and not a drop to drink

DOS, DOS don't you know the road

What I've never understood about fashion is that
if you buy a new swimsuit (what we used to call
bathing suit) every summer what do you do with
the old trunks?

Où sont les bikinis *d'antan?*

"Yeah yeah" [negative double positive]

MAKE MAYONNAISE NOT MUNITIONS

DISPOSSESS THE RICH NOT THE POOR

Save gas, stay at home.
Save electricity, sleep more.
Improve your mind, get a vasectomy.

No I'm not hostile, just unhappy.

No I'm not unhappy, just hostile.

I mean, *hospitable* . . . I mean I've been
a little grumpy the past few decades

Harder for a rich man to read a poem than
for a hippopotamus to sing bel canto.

Preposterous!

Para(pa)posterous.

Indubitably, indubitablier, emergency intubation

—But then you've probably never heard Rataxes sing!

Not only that, either—when two bits ain't
worth a dime, you might as well swap those
Swamis for some canned fish

No, I'm not sarcastic, just unsettled, like
images of the Indians trouble my sleep, like
we settled altogether too much too fast &
have to throw out our backs retracing our
steps

There is a madness to their method: Take no
prisoners, pensioners

For to dissect is to delight in the
sentient; all else is so much hocus
pocus, ring-a-levios of repression and
triplebind, culpable blindness to what
is before our touch. Read to redress,
disguise as promise—not to submit.

Hollow words with a ring of truth,
signet of sorrow. Not to reprimand is
to be remanded to the custody of those
escaped the tide of moral pull:
accumulation beyond the wildest needs
of child or woman or man—this is
the first sin. Our jailers
are our constipating sense of self—
not that madmen claim many kin.
Rue or be ruled or take a ruler
to the wind to measure the gravity
that locates us surely as the morning
falls, whether or not we get up.

Or else—

wake me for meals

THE INFLUENCE OF KINSHIP PATTERNS UPON PERCEPTION OF AN AMBIGUOUS STIMULUS

What's money worth? Not a whole lot if
You come up a few bits short & come
Away empty handed. If that was the case
What would you have to say then? At least
The motorperson knows how to blow a whistle.
At least in the winter it's not summer
(God damn mosquitoes & horseflies). What did
The Mandela say to the Mandela? BOY
HITS IGLOO. Snowed motion, i.e., frosted or
Laminated. To be such a bitter pill
& have nothing wrong. *Don't laugh*
It really hurted. If you put on
My shirt then what shirt am I
Going to wear? The kind of people
Wear plaid Bermuda shorts. The kind of
People that judge people who wear

Plaid Bermuda shorts. The kind of

Day this has been (I think I am

Falling into a tunnel of love but

Forget to get on). For a long time I'd

Say *twirl* when I meant 'spin'. Have you

Heard the one about the fly & the

Paper? The fly bottle could not found

The fly. The Mother Bear could not

Find the rest of the story. Harry has his

Troubles too but these are not interesting enough

To bear replay. "That's a very

Suspicious-looking baby." "It's hard

Not to be a baby." "But

Are there really babies or just baby-

Behavior?" —For the purpose

Of your request I'm including this

Sentence about the influence of John

Ashbery. While the packet

Boat sunk I can still imagine I am

Crawling into it; at the same time the ice

Is too thin to

Pretend to fall through.

Meanwhile, the water is wetter in the

Rich man's pond but doesn't taste

As good. —Hey wait a minute!

That's a bit *too* close, try to stay

Back *at least 10* inches. So what

If the margins don't

Turn out right? Whadda you *mean* you're

Going to the next poem? *This is the best*

Part! Oh, I'm sorry, I guess I misunderstood

You. —But nobody seems to want to hear

About the pain we men feel

Having our prerogatives questioned.

A bunch of darn-dash pragmatists

With justice on their side (for all

The good that will do them). Don't

Frame me or I'll bust you in the

Doldrums. —*Now let's*

Switch the subject & try to find

Out what's on *your* mind. Voyage of life

Getting you down? Felt better when things

Were really rocky & now there's smooth

Sailing but it's lost its meaning? I'm a

Good listener & only mildly demanding:

There's just the one-time fee (mostly

For paper & printing & distribution

Costs) & unlimited returns. I'm bubbling over

With empathy & good advice & I'm not

Afraid to tell you where I think you've

Gone wrong. Let's face it—

From the word *go* you've

Resented me—resented my being finished

In the face of your—what?—continuing

On? But I don't mean to be complete

If that makes you feel distant; still

As I say, I

Do want some distance. She was a

Sort of Betsy Ross figure but without the

Accoutrements—no washer/dryer, just the one

TV. I said to her—What can you *expect*

From a poem?—evidently a lot less than

She did. A poem bleeds

Metaphorically, just like I do. I can

No more breathe than face

The music. But if the first

Banana smells a rat look out for

Lost leader (tossed reader). —"I

don't think I'm ever

Going home." —I don't think

I've ever been home. *We are looking for*

Cheerful, enthusiastic self-starters

With solid backgrounds in detailed

Wails. The point

Not to change history but to change

Events. For instance, you

Can change in the car, change on the

Beach, or use a changing room

At the beach. Don't change me

& I won't change a hair on your

Chinny chin chin. Or let me

Put it this way: You can call

Me anything you want to but give me

The right change. That's right: I

haven't changed, you have. It's

Not the time it's the beer. I'm in

A rush, don't forget to send a

Check. Not a con

Just a dodge. Not a dodge a Lincoln-

Mercury. *Take me to your leader.* Take me

To the 5 & Dime I've got to go.

Faith under leisure: as difficult as

Keeping a hat in a hurricane

Or an appointment with an erasure.

One Mandela hit the other Mandela in the nose.

What color blood came out?

R - E - D spells *red.*

Are you people? You're about the nicest people

I know & I know some pretty unpleasant

characters.

DARK CITY

We're a great pair—
I've got no voice
& you've got no ear.
   —LIZABETH SCOTT TO
   CHARLTON HESTON, *Dark City*

1. APPLE-PICKING TIME

A transom stands bound to a flagpole. Hard
by we go hardly which way is which
lingering somewhere unsettled where evidence
comes harder by sockets, stems
etched in flexed omission like osmotic
molarities flickering edge and orange at flow
rates unrepresentative of ticking or torpor
any child or person requires for, well
against, that remorse remonstration
brings. It's cold outside, maybe
but the heart sinks daily in
slump of sampled parts and *I*
feel like carelessness, disowning what's
acquired in indifferent
animation, no body swaps to—
not as if elevated or cut down

to size up, like layers of lost
boys, like aspiration in a tub
at sea, lists all the scores and
scares at measures twice the fall.
I'm parked because I have no taste
to go—penned down, no row to call
my own. *Abruptly, silently* borrowing
ignition from rumble, pouring
face into a
stir . . .
We're a great fire, pining for a
tower to burn through, yet no matter
whose ice scatters our shouts—
dive for the switches, bury the
slots.

> There's an eggplant in heaven
> Seen it there, know the sign
> It's awaiting for me
> End of time, long-lost rime

I loved my love with gold
She loved me with her smile
But I took no possession
Then / Had no taste called mine
I knew I wept alone that night
As sure as sheep in folds

The I has ways the arm betrays
For now my lance is warped

The Bitter Core o'erwhelms its fate
An abler loss casts breeze
Sobriety's a fool's way out
I'll take the sea in me, in me
Nor swap the waves for thee.

Floorlength gowns of commodious indelicacy
suffusing articles on plums
in monk's applause, equipped with attenuated
slips, adjunctive rumination, felt
bellows. Before I, in the interests of
but not to further ascribe, at which
mechanism, slate, pediment, protrusion
abutment, laceration, absinthe-oriented
divestment gaged to occur or unveil
its numinous ectoplasmic Jill or gel or
JELLO AGAIN THIS IS JACK BENNY FOR
JELLO PUDDING AND PIE FILLING.
Overboard or just over-by-a-long
shot. Grateful to even imagine
shore.

　　　As a matter of fact
　　　I'm as good as packed.

I slept longer than you
Now isn't that true?

A poem should not mean but impale
not be but bemoan,

                              boomerang
buck(le)
        bubble. Malted meadows & hazelnut
innuendos: I'll bet the soda water
gets the shakes sooner than
Dan gets to Tampa. "Don't Tampa
with me or I'll lacerate that
evisceration off your face so fast
you'll think my caddle prod was a
lollipop." "Stay out my face or I'll
deploy my assets against whatever
collateral you've got left after I
target your abstemious alarm." He
was the kind of guy who pushed
my buttons but couldn't carry a
tune from Kuala Lumpur to
Guadalajara, like those zebras
with cross hatchings, or the trapeze
family with Venusian ventilators. I
mean I felt good at first
but then it dawned on me, what
if it was really a mistake, maybe

I shouldn't have said what I
said, did what I
done. Mildred paced around the museum
for another few hours before she spotted
him, but it was much too crowded to
finish the job right there. "They were
my favorite boots," she cried. "They are
your only boots," I replied.

2. EARLY FROST

I think it's time we let the cat out
its bag, swung the dog over the
shoulder, so to say, let the hens
say "hey" to the woodpeckers, doled
out some omniaversions to the
too-tapped-upon, the tethers without
toggles, the field-happy expeditioneers
on the march to Tuscaloosa, Beloit,
Manual Falls, Florid Oasis.
"Damn but you're a beautiful
cow / of a / bell! Haven't
I seen you on the radio?"
Where are those fades (arcades, shades)
when you need them? Who
was that text I saw you with

last night? Is there life after
grammar (glamour)? The Czech
is in the jail (the wreck is
in the wail, the deck is in the
sail, the Burma-Shave's shining over the
starry blue skies, Waukegan, New Jersey,
1941). *He that cannot pay: let him pay!*
She that peeps through a hole will kiss
the wave that troubled her. No larder
but has its puddle, no rose without
overthrows. Ask no questions and at last
you shall be blind! A stumble may
prevent a fall but a fall guy's
my kind of man. Every poem
has its price, every anxiety its reward—
but no person ever tripped in the same
place more than *I* choose to
recall. There are spots even on the
sofa (meddle not with another person's
meddling, i.e., the rock that falls
from the sky breaks your toes).
For the footprint makes the joint a
well-appointed appurtenance aside the
jesting hooligan, shenanigan, or
general call to bedlam, or did
she say, *be calm*? Clammy hands
hurt the advancement of the waiter

but I never heard no tell of no
gust or gallon of time worth the
curing in weight alone. Boxers
can't live by punching alone, but
stay clear of such as possible—a
Divine Swerve will still land you
in Hell's cauldron. *Thus*
make your peace with yourself at
your own risk for peace with the Devil
costs everybody more than you could
hope to destroy. *Holy is as holy does.*
Essence precludes existence.

3. ENDLESS DESTINATION

If I should die
cut out my throat
and burn it on the pyre
of their indifference.
It means no more to me
than that, to take
your hand in my
hand and turn our backs
from the wreck
not of our lives
but where we have been given

to live them. I would not
walk alone here, where the
dark surrounds, where your face
radiates beyond my swollen
misgivings and clarifies the mist
of my belonging. Stay near
that I may hold you lightly
else the fear inside tear
away what measures I have
held against the night.

Love's no more than that
a straw against the wind
that blows us to the ground
without submission. Come
love, come, take this
shadow I call me: cast
it against stone, lest the gloom
become us. Come cast me
down 'gainst shore, where
sand enfolds us.

Love is like love, a baby
like a baby, meaning like
memory, light like light.
A journey's a detour
and a pocket a charm

in which deceits are borne.
A cloud is a cloud and
a story like a story,
song is a song, fury
like fury.

4. IN THE PINK

Now let's turn to some advice for expectant
fathers. Never wear a hat to a
hanging or carry a feather pillow to
cello practice. Suffer not the
professor of culture nor the minister
of taste, but assail all who
complacent sit in the place of those
deserve it. Take the cracks on
the wall as your credo or call—
obscurity's in the eye of
ones will not behold—
what they can understand
isn't worth the price of
a used tin can. I may be loco
but at least I listen: What
you've tuned out would make a Paradise
of Plies.

This is the difference between truth
and reality: the one advertises itself
in the court of brute circumstance
the other is framed by its own
insistences. Truth's religious, reality
cultural, or rather
truth is the ground of reality's
appearance but reality intervenes
against all odds.

5. THE PLIGHT OF THE BUMBLEBEE

She was a rudder
without anchor
in a chaos
of expectation,
a comb
without teeth, a
brush without
bristles.

6. [UNTITLED]

"The words
come out of

her heart
& into the
language"
& the language
is in the heart
of that girl
who is in the heart
of you.

A DEFENCE OF POETRY

FOR BRIAN MCHALE

My problem with deploying a term liek
nonelen
in these cases is acutually similar to
your
cirtique of the term ideopigical
unamlsing as a too-broad unanuajce
interprestive proacdeure.
You say too musch lie a steamroller when
we need dental (I;d say jeweller's)
tools.
(I thin youy misinterpret the natuer of
some of the poltical claims go; not
themaic
interpretatiomn of evey
evey detail in every peim
but an oeitnetation towatd a kind of
texutal practice
that you prefer to call "nknsense" but
for *poltical* purpses I prepfer to call
ideological!
, say Hupty Dumpty)
Taht is, nonesene see,msm to reduce a

vareity of fieefernt
prosdodic, thematic and discusrive
enactcemnts into a zeroo degree of
sense. What we have is a vareity of
valences. Nin-sene.sense is too binary
andoppostioin, too much oall or nithing
account with ninesense seeming by its
very meaing to equl no sense at all. We
have preshpas a blurrig of sense, whih
means not relying on convnetionally
methods of *conveying* sense but whih may
aloow for dar greater sense-smakinh than
specisigusforms of doinat disoucrse that
makes no sense at all by irute of thier
hyperconventionality (Bush's speeches,
calssically). Indeed you say that
nonsenese shed leds on its "antithesis"
sense making: but teally the antithsisi
of these poems you call nonselnse is not
sense-making itslef but perhps, in some
cases, the simulation of sense-making:
decitfullness, manifpulation, the
media-ization of language, etc.
I don't agree with Stewart that "the
more exptreme the disontinuities . . . the
more nonsisincial" : I hear sense
beginning to made in this sinstances.

Te probelm though is the definaitonof
sense. What you mean by nomsense is
soething like a-rational, but ratio (and
this goes back to Blake not to meanion
the pre-Socaratics) DOES NOT EQUAL
sense! This realtioes to the sort of
oscillation udnertood as rhytmic or
prosidci, that I disusccio in Artiofice.
Crucialy, the duck/rabitt exmaple is one
of the ambiguity of *aspects* and clearly
not a bprobelm of noneselnse: tjere are
two competing, completely sensible,
readings, not even any blurring; the
issue is context-depednece)otr
apsrevcyt blindness as Witegenstein
Nonesesen is too static. Deosnt't
Prdunne even say int e eoem "sense occurs
"at the contre-coup:: in the process of
oscillatio itself.
b6y the waylines 9–10 are based on an
aphorism by Karl Kraus: *the closer we
look at a word the greater the distance
from which it stares back.*

DEAR MR. FANELLI,

I saw your picture
in the 79th street
station. You said
you'd be interested
in any comments I
might have on the
condition of the
station. Mr. Fanelli,
there is a lot of
debris in the 79th street
station that makes it
unpleasant to wait in
for more than a few
minutes. The station
could use a paint
job and maybe
new speakers so you
could understand
the delay announcements
that are always being
broadcast. Mr.
Fanelli—there are
a lot of people sleeping
in the 79th street station

& it makes me sad
to think they have no
home to go to. Mr.
Fanelli, do you think
you could find a more
comfortable place for them
to rest? It's pretty noisy
in the subway, especially with
all those express trains
hurtling through every
few minutes, anyway when the
trains are in service.
I have to admit, Mr. Fanelli, I
think the 79th street station's
in pretty bad shape
& sometimes at night
as I toss in my bed
I think the world's
not doing too good
either, & I
wonder what's going
to happen, where we're
headed, if we're
headed anywhere, if
we even have heads. Mr.
Fanelli, do you think if
we could just start

with the 79th street
station & do what
we could with that
then maybe we could,
you know, I guess, move
on from there? Mr.
Fanelli, when I saw your
picture & the sign
asking for suggestions
I thought, if
you really wanted to
get to the bottom
of what's wrong then
maybe it was my job
to write you: Maybe
you've never been inside
the 79th street station
because you're so busy
managing the 72nd street
& 66th street stations,
maybe you don't know
the problems we have
at 79th—I mean the
dirt & frequent
delays & the feeling of
total misery that
pervades the place. Mr.

Fanelli, are you reading
this far in the letter
or do you get so
many letters every day
that you don't have
time to give each
one the close attention
it desires? Or am I
the only person who's
taken up your invitation
to get in touch &
you just don't have enough
experience to know how to
respond? I'm sorry
I can't get your attention
Mr. Fanelli because I really
believe if you ask
for comments then you
ought to be willing
to act on them—even
if *ought* is too
big a word to throw
around at this point.
Mr. Fanelli
I hope you won't
think I'm rude
if I ask you a

personal question. Do
you get out of the
office much?
Do you go to the movies
or do you prefer
sports—or maybe
quiet evenings at a
local restaurant? Do
you read much, Mr. Fanelli?
I don't mean just
Gibbon and like
that, but philosophy—
have you read much
Hannah Arendt or
do you prefer
a more ideological
perspective?
I think if I understood
where you're coming from,
Mr. Fanelli, I could
write to you more cogently,
more persuasively. Mr.
Fanelli, do you get out
of the city at all—I
mean like up to Bear
Mountain or out to
Montauk? I mean do you

notice how unpleasant
the air is in the 79th
street station—that we
could use some cooling
or air-filtering system
down there? Mr.
Fanelli, do you think
it's possible we
could get together
and talk about
these things in
person? There are
a few other points
I'd like to go over
with you if I could
get the chance. Things
I'd like to talk to
you about but that
I'd be reluctant to
put down on paper.
Mr. Fanelli, I haven't
been feeling very good
lately and I thought
meeting with you face
to face might change
my mood, might put
me into a new frame

of mind. Maybe we
could have lunch?
Or maybe after work?
Think about it, Mr.
Fanelli.

SOLIDARITY IS THE NAME WE GIVE TO WHAT WE CANNOT HOLD

I am a nude formalist poet, a sprung
syntax poet, a multitrack poet, a
wondering poet, a social expressionist
poet, a Baroque poet, a constructivist poet,
an ideolectical poet. I am a New York poet in
California, a San Francisco poet on
the Lower East Side, an Objectivist poet
in Royaumont, a surrealist poet in Jersey,
a Dada poet in Harvard Square,
a zaum poet in Brooklyn, a merz poet
in Iowa, a cubo-futurist poet in Central Park.
I am a Buffalo poet in Providence, a London
poet in Cambridge, a Kootenay School
of Writing poet in Montreal, a local poet
in Honolulu.
I am a leftist poet in my armchair
and an existential poet on the street;
an insider poet among my friends,
an outsider poet in midtown.
I am a serial poet, a paratactic poet, a
disjunctive poet, a discombobulating poet,
a montage poet, a collage poet, a hypertextual
poet, a nonlinear poet, an abstract poet,

a nonrepresentational poet, a process poet,
a polydiscourse poet, a conceptual poet.
I am a vernacular poet, a talk poet, a dialect
poet, a heteroglossic poet, a slang poet, a
demotic poet, a punning poet, a comic poet.
I am an iambic poet I am,
a dactylic poet, a tetrameter poet,
an anapestic poet.
I am a capitalist poet in Leningrad
and a socialist poet in St. Petersburg;
a bourgeois poet at Zabar's, a union poet
in Albany; an elitist poet on TV,
a political poet on the radio.
I am a fraudulent poet, an incomprehensible poet, a degenerate
poet, an incompetent poet, an indecorousness poet, a crude poet
an incoherent poet, a flat-footed poet, a disruptive poet, a
fragmenting poet, a contradictory poet, a self-imploding poet,
a conspiratorial poet, an ungainly poet, an anti-dogmatic poet,
an infantile poet, a theoretical poet, an awkward poet, a sissy
poet, an egghead poet, a perverse poet, a clumsy poet,
a cacophonous poet, a vulgar poet, a warped
poet, a silly poet, a queer poet, an
erratic poet, an erroneous poet, an anarchic poet,
a cerebral poet, an unruly poet,
an emotional poet, a (no) nonsense poet. I am a language
poet wherever people try to limit the modes of
expression or nonexpression. I am an experimental poet
to those who value craft over interrogation, an

avant-garde poet to those who see the future

in the present. I am a Jewish poet hiding in the shadow

of my great-grandfather and great-grandmother.

I am a difficult poet in Kent, a visual poet in

Cleveland, a sound poet in Cincinnati.

I am a modernist poet to postmodernists and a postmodern poet

to modernists. I am a book artist in Minneapolis

and a language artist in Del Mar.

I am a lyric poet in Spokane, an analytic

poet in South Bend, a narrative poet

in Yellowknife, a realist

poet in Berkeley.

I am an antiabsorptive poet in the morning,

an absorptive poet in the afternoon,

and a sleepy poet at night.

I am a parent poet, a white poet, a man poet, an urban poet,

    an angered poet, a sad poet,

an elegiac poet, a raucous poet, a frivolous poet, a detached poet,

    a roller-coaster poet, a

volcanic poet, a dark poet, a skeptical poet, an eccentric poet,

    a misguided poet, a reflective

poet, a dialectical poet, a polyphonic poet, a hybrid poet,

    a wandering poet, an odd poet, a

lost poet, a disobedient poet, a bald poet, a virtual poet.

& I am none of these things,

nothing but the blank wall of my aversions

writ large in disappearing ink —

GERTRUDE AND LUDWIG'S
BOGUS ADVENTURE

FOR GABRIELE MINTZ

As Billy goes higher all the balloons
Get marooned on the other side of the
Lunar landscape. The module's broke—
It seems like for an eternity, but who's
Counting—and Sally's joined the Moonies
So we don't see so much of her anyhow.
Notorious novelty—I'd settle for a good
Cup of Chase & Sand-borne—though when
The strings are broken on the guitar
You can always use it as a coffee table.
Vienna was cold at that time of year.
The sachertorte tasted sweet but the memory
burned in the colon. Get a grip, get a grip, before
The Grippe gets you. Glad to see the picture
Of ink—the pitcher that pours before
Throwing the Ball, with never a catcher in sight.
Never a catcher but sometimes a catch, or
A clinch or a clutch or a spoon—never a
Catcher but plenty o' flack, 'til we meet
On this side of the tune.

A TEST OF POETRY

What do you mean by *rashes of ash*? Is *industry*
systematic work, assiduous activity, or ownership
of factories? Is *ripple* agitate lightly? Are
we *tossed in tune* when we write poems? And
what or who *emboss with gloss insignias of air*?

Is the *Fabric* about which you write in the epigraph
of your poem an edifice, a symbol of heaven?

Does *freight* refer to cargo or lading carried
for pay by water, land or air? Or does it mean
payment for such transportation? Or a freight
train? When you say a *commoded journey*,
do you mean a comfortable journey or a good train
with well-equipped commodities? But, then, why
do you drop the 'a' before *slumberous friend*? And
when you write, in "Why I Am Not a Christian"
*You always throw it down / But you never
pick it up*—what is *it*?

In "The Harbor of Illusion", does *vein*
refer to a person's vein under his skin or
is it a metaphor for a river? Does *lot*
mean one's fate or a piece of land?

And does *camphor* refer to camphor trees?
Moreover, who or what is *nearing*. Who or
what has *fell*? Or does *fell* refer to the
skin or hide of an animal? And who or what has
stalled? Then, is the *thoroughfare of
noon's atoll* an equivalent of *the template*?

In "Fear of Flipping" does *flipping* mean
crazy?

How about *strain*, does it mean
a severe trying or wearing pressure or
effect (such as a strain of hard work),
or a passage, as in piece of music?
Does *Mercury* refer to a brand of oil?

In the lines
*shards of bucolic pastry anchored
against cactus cabinets, Nantucket buckets*
could we take it as—pieces of pies
or tarts are placed in buckets (which
are made of wood from Nantucket)
anchored against cabinets (small
rooms or furniture?) with cactus?

What is *nutflack*?

I suppose the *caucus of caucasians*
refers to the white people's meeting
of a political party to nominate candidates.
But who is Uncle Hodgepodge?
And what does *familiar freight*
to the returning antelope mean?

You write, *the walls are our floors.*
How can the *walls* be floors if the floors
refer to the part of the room which forms
its enclosing surface and upon which one
walks? In *and the floors, like balls,*
repel all falls—does *balls* refer to
nonsense or to any ball like a basket ball
or to guys? Or to a social assembly for
dancing? *Falls* means to descend
from a higher to a lower
or to drop down wounded or dead?
But what is *the so-called overall*
mesh?

Is the *garbage heap* the garbage heap
in the ordinary sense? Why does
garbage heap exchange for *so-called*
overall mesh? Since a *faker* is
one who fakes, how can
arbitrary reduce to *faker*?

Who or what are disappointed
not to have been?

Does *frames* refer to form, constitution,
or structure in general? Or to a
particular state, as of the mind?

In the sentence,
*If you don't like it
colored in, you can always xerox it
and see it all gray*
—what is *it*? What does
colored in mean?

A few lines later you write,
You mean, image farm when you've got bratwurst—
Does *bratwurst* refer to sausage?
Does the line mean—the sausage
you saw reminded you of a farm which you imagined?

Does *fat-bottom boats* refer to boats with thick bottoms?
Is *humble then humped* used to describe the actions of one
who plays golf? In the phrase *a sideshow freak—*
the *freak* refers to a hippie? *Sideshow* refers to secondary
importance? Or an abnormal actor in the sideshow?
Then, who or what is *linked* with *steam of pink.* And
how about *the tongue-tied tightrope stalker—*

does the *stalker* refer to one who is pursuing
stealthily in the act of hunting game? The stalker
is a witness at first and then a witless witness?

You write *The husks are salted*:
what kind of nut husks can be salted for eating?
What does *bending* mean—to become curved,
crooked, or bent? Or to bow down in submission
or reverence, yield, submit? Does *bells*
refer to metallic sounding instruments or
a kind of trousers?

Just a few lines later you have the phrase
Felt very poured. Who felt poured? Toys?
Is *humming* in the sense of humming a song?
Stepped into where? *Not being part of* what?

In "No Pastrami" (*Walt! I'm with you in Sydney/Where
the echoes of Mamaroneck howl/Down the outback's
pixilating corridors*)—does the *pastrami* refer
to a highly seasoned shoulder cut of beef? Is
Mamaroneck a place in the U.S. where wild oxes howl?
I take it *corridors* refers to the passageway
in the supermarket? Could I read the poem as—
The speaker is doing shopping in a supermarket
in Sydney; he is walking along the eccentric
passageways among the shelves on which goods

are placed; he does not want to buy the pastrami
as he seems to have heard the echoes of wild oxes
howling in the U.S. while he addresses Walt Whitman?

In *No end to envy*, does the envy refer to admire or
in the bad sense?

This line is stripped of emotion.
This line is no more than an
illustration of a European
theory. This line is bereft
of a subject. This line
has no reference apart
from its context in
this line. This line
is only about itself.
This line has no meaning:
its words are imaginary, its
sounds inaudible. This line
cares not for itself or for
anyone else—it is indifferent,
impersonal, cold, uninviting.
This line is elitist, requiring,
to understand it, years of study
in stultifying libraries, poring
over esoteric treatises on
impossible to pronounce topics.
This line refuses reality.

RIDDLE

What falls on air yet's lighter
than balloon? What betrays time
yet folds into a cut? Who flutters
at the sight of song then bellows
into flight? What height is
halved by precipice, what gorge
dissolved by trill? Who telling
tales upbraids a stump when
prattle veils its want?

Stone breaks it not, nor diamonds,
yet splits with just one word: it's
used for casting devils out; still,
fools obey it first.

MAO TSE TUNG WORE KHAKIS

Who would have thought Paul McCartney would be
the Perry Como of the 1990s?
The Thunderbirds gleam end-to-end-to-end
in the studio backlot. The lions
have left their lair and are roaming just by
the subconscious. PP-warning: Illegal
received field on preceding line.
Bethel/'94: I just don't want any
hippies come in here and steal
my computer. *In my experience*
I often misspell words. Evidently
Bob Dylan missed the exit and ended
up in Saugerties. You can sell some of
the people most of the time, but you can't

LIFTJAR AGATE

1   "I hate that you blame me For

2   the things I do wrong" A pear

3   would go to heaven As easily as

4   a blade of grass Would sing your

5   song. But the notice, she is given

6   The Sway outlasts the throng In the

7   nabbing there's More to pay Than circuits

8   in a barn. You know that time,

9   years ago If chance allots recall, The

10   bluff fell down You fussed, I frowned

11   But where those yesterdays In the

12   musty torpors of Tomorrows? Green glides

13   the fence Red knows the door

14   A switch is heavier When the

15   bolting soars. A foxy boy a

16   fool becomes When manner glides &

17   Furor's none. Forsake the swaddle, curdle

18   the door You'll still be a

19   version When yearnings link In thrall.

There is no shade in the forest
when we beat our wings against the moss
& tear the petals off the spruce
revealing what's never said but
spoken, companion to discordant facts
stacked three-foot high above the drawers
clogging corridors. Consonance is this
world's only comfort, stony stare of
stars on bleary night, awake enough
to lose a dozen threads, invent a baker's
dozen more for recompense. The gravel
does not hold, the road beyond repair,
yet closer to, by far, than dusk's approaching
glare.

AFTER CAMPION

It was on a summer's day
Found myself alone and gray

When Susan began to speak
On the road in front of me

First she dodged, then she spun
Bells were ringing I heard some

Emma sang then twice complained
She was in the mood to reign

Felix woke, he sang too
Had no idea what to do

Music strays, will's composed
Pleasure strikes when feeling stays

Blessed are the narrow who slide
among cracks and build monuments to
slats. For long have I awaited
such news as now passes comment—
news of my comrades lost long
at sea. It was in the following winter
that word was received in a foreign
tongue that one who had refused
solace for some these fifteen months
had taken the hand of his born
foe and danced the Hokey Pokey with
the abandon of clues at
sunset. Such light that fails
me, like sticks in mission
sand, voracious melody of
hardly heard vibrations, potable
allegiance subsumed in the tube.

RIVULETS OF THE DEAD JEW

Fill my plate with *boudin noir*
Boudin noir, boudin noir
Fill my plate with a hi-heh-ho
& rumble I will go

Don't dance with me
'til I cut my tie
Cut my tie, cut my tie
Don't fancy me 'til
The rivers run dry
& a heh & a hi & a ho

I've got a date with a
Bumble bee, bumble bee
I've got a date with a
wee bonnie wee
& ahurtling we will go

DOGGY BAG

FOR OLIVIER CADIOT

have you seen my doggy bag
hate to nag, hate to nag
have you seen my emerald chain
hate to brag, hate to brag

I ate the supper in the village
lunch at the lodge
if you don't give me back my
upper teeth
I am going to drool like a

man that once had silver
man that once had gold
man that once had everything
but a tune of his own

so have you seen my nodding mare
my lurking pony, my sultry donkey
have you seen my cuts and jags
hate to frag, hate to frag
have you seen my broken drum
hate to gab, hate to gab

the toilet seat is down now
it's there I plan to sit
until I find that doggy bag
I lost while just a kid

THE BOY SOPRANO

Daddy loves me this I know
Cause my granddad told me so
Though he beats me blue and black
That's because I'm full of crap

My mommy she is ultra cool
Taught me the Bible's golden rule
Don't talk back, do what you're told
Abject compliance is as good as gold

The teachers teach the grandest things
Tell how poetry's words on wings
But wings are for Heaven, not for earth
Want my advice: hijack the hearse

JOHNNY CAKE HOLLOW

Xo quwollen swacked unt myrry flooped
Sardone to fligrunt's swirm, ort
Jirmy plaight org garvey swait ib
Giben durrs urk klurpf. Sheb
Boughtie bloor de dazzy dule dun
Fruppi's ghigo's gly, jud
Chyllrophane jed jimmsy's cack—
Exenst aerodole fump glire. Eb
Horray bloot, ig orry sluit neb
Nist neb ot neb gwon. Shleb
Atsum imba outsey burft allappie
Merp av ords. Een ainsey swish
Ien ansley sploop ughalls dep dulster
Flooge, ig ahrs unt nimbet twool
Begroob, ig ooburs quwate ag blurg.

THIS POEM INTENTIONALLY LEFT BLANK

MEMORIES

1. GRANDFATHERS

The farm never seemed the same after Gramps died
Grace kept saying, "Every life has its tide"
But to have his testicles cut that way
Even if he had done what, whatever they say

The corn grew high as a boy in britches
I loved the smell of the bulls and bitches
Motorcars and kikes seemed a world away
We thought we would always lounge in the hay

The first time I was in Kansas City
All the boys and girls looked so damn pretty
I said to my great friend, hey Joe, I said
How come Gramps said we'd be better off dead

Than drinkin' the sweet liquor and tasting the fruits—
The muscles and turnips and duckling soups
Such that we never ever none did had
When, oh when, we were tiny lads

2. HERITAGE

Don't you steal that flag, my Mama had qualms
But a boy gotta have something to boast on
Crack that rock, slit that toad
Nature's a hoot if you shoot your load

Flies in the oven
Flies in the head
I'll kill that fly
Till I kill it dead
And no more will that fly
Bother me
As I roam and I ramble
In the tumbleweed

3. TOUGH LOVE

My Dad and I were very close
I like to say, int'mately gruff:
We hunted bear, skinned slithy toes
You know, played ball and all that stuff.
Daddy had his pride and maybe was aloof
But when he hit me, that was proof—
Proof that he cared
More than he could ever share.

How I hated those men who took him away!
Pop was a passionate man
Just like me
And I'll teach my son, Clem
To love just like we men.

4. SISTERS

William Kennedy Smith
He is an honorable man
And Mike Tyson's
A giant in my clan.
The liberals and the fem'nists
Hate men and vivisectionists.
But when they want the garbage out
Who do they ask, we guys no doubt.

What do you see, Nonny?
What do you see?
A tune & a stain
Waiting for me

Will you go there, Nonny?
Will you go there?
It's just by the corner
Right over the bend

Who'll you see there, Nonny?
Who'll you see there?
A monkey, a merchant, a pixelated man

What will you say, Nonny?
What will you say?
I'm just a nobody making my way

IN PARTICULAR

I admit that beauty inhales me but not that I inhale beauty
— FELIX BERNSTEIN

My lack of nothingness
— THE GENIE IN THE CANDY STORE

A black man waiting at a bus stop
A white woman sitting on a stool
A Filipino eating a potato
A Mexican boy putting on shoes
A Hindu hiding in igloo
A fat girl in blue blouse
A Christian lady with toupee
A Chinese mother walking across a bridge
An Afghanistani eating pastrami
A provincial walking on the peninsula
A Eurasian boy on a cell phone
An Arab with umbrella
A Southerner taking off a backpack
An Italian detonating a land line
A barbarian with beret
A Lebanese guy in limousine
A Jew watering petunias
A Yugoslavian man at a hanging
A Sunni boy on scooter

A Floridian climbing a fountain

A Beatnik writing a limerick

A Caucasian woman dreaming of indecision

A Puerto Rican child floating on a balloon

An Indian fellow gliding on three-wheeled bike

An Armenian rowing to Amenia

An Irish lad with scythe

A Bangladeshi muttering questions

A worker wading in puddles

A Japanese rollerblader fixing a blend

A Burgundian tailor watching his trailer

An Idaho man getting a tan

A Quinnipiac girl with a bluesy drawl

An Arapahoe whaler skimming failure

An anorexic man with a remarkably deep tan

An adolescent Muslim writing terza rima

A Scots pipe fitter at the automat

A gay guy in tweed boat

A red man with green ball

A dyslexic sailor with an inconsolable grin

A Northumbrian flier heading for Tipperary

A Buddhist financier falling to ground

A curious old boy jumping into threshing machine

An Hispanic sergeant on lookout for a cream-colored coat

An addicted haberdasher eating soap

A Peruvian child chewing gum

A Sephardic infant on shuffleboard deck

A Mongolian imitating Napoleon

An anarchist lad with skewed glance

A Latvian miner break dancing with the coroner

A poor girl eating apple pie and cream soda

A Sudanese fellow with a yellow stroller

An atheist with a flare for pins

A Bahamanian on the way to inordinate machination

A stuttering Iranian in blue and gold fog

A tell-tale somnambulist rehearsing *Gypsy*

A homosexual child in a taxi

A Wiccan matron swimming in glue

A Moravian procrastinator practicing jujitsu

A Syrian swami on Lake Oragami

A flirtatious gentleman spinning wool

A colored youngster admiring a toaster

A Danish designer in a diner

A Montenegrin taking Excedrin

A D.C. dervish dribbling dodecahedrons

A Denver doyen davening defiantly

A Bali busboy getting high

An Iraqi contemplating hari-kari

An Ojibwa pushing a button on the Trans-Siberian

A harried officer somersaulting on banister

A moldy Whig directing catfish

An agoraphobic professor on cruise control

A feminist in a rocking chair

A Botswanan cook in bobby socks

A teenager infiltrating an air mattress

A pro-choice guy reciting rimes

A dog-faced Finn in shining car

A Czech man in a check suit

A Pentecostal lawyer jogging in his foyer

A communist wearing a sad apron

A Canadian woman with a nose ring

A ghoulish girl dating a dentist

An idiot in a closet

A Moorish magician in her kitchen

A sorrowful soldier with a morose clothier

A dilettantish senior washing strictures

A socialite on routine imbroglio

A bicyclist hoarding hornets

A toddler pocketing the till

A hooded boy eating cheddar cheese

A balding brownnoser in tutu

A brunette chasing choo-choo train

An Argentine dancing on a dime

A bespeckled dowager installing Laplink

An australopithecine toddler grimacing in basement

A Nicaraguan pee-wee with preposterous pipe

A kike out cold on ice

A Hoosier off the booze

A swollen man with an impecunious grin

A Burmese fellow with face of terror

A lost poll in the forest

A dilapidated soul drinking rum

A pistolero with folded heart

A Shockwave momma hunkering down on puck

A vellobound baby two-facing the cha-cha

A postcolonial fiduciary eating a plum

A maladroit Swede coughing bullets

A hexed Haitian on involuntary vacation

A Persian oncologist in metrical parking

A Peruvian French hornist sipping Pernod

A Terre Haute charmer with infinite capacity to harm her

A Mongolian chiropodist at a potluck

A São Paulo poet reflecting on deflection

A white man sitting on stool

A black woman waiting at bus stop

THANK YOU FOR SAYING THANK YOU

This is a totally
accessible poem.
There is nothing
in this poem
that is in any
way difficult
to understand.
All the words
are simple &
to the point.
There are no new
concepts, no
theories, no
ideas to confuse
you. This poem
has no intellectual
pretensions. It is
purely emotional.
It fully expresses
the feelings of the
author: *my feelings,*
the person speaking
to you now.
It is all about

communication.
Heart to heart.
This poem appreciates
& values you as
a reader. It
celebrates the
triumph of the
human imagination
amidst pitfalls &
calamities. This poem
has 90 lines,
269 words, and
more syllables than
I have time to
count. Each line,
word, & syllable
has been chosen
to convey only the
intended meaning
& nothing more.
This poem abjures
obscurity & enigma.
There is nothing
hidden. A hundred
readers would each
read the poem
in an identical

manner & derive
the same message
from it. This
poem, like all
good poems, tells
a story in a direct
style that never
leaves the reader
guessing. While
at times expressing
bitterness, anger,
resentment, xenophobia,
& hints of racism, its
ultimate mood is
affirmative. It finds
joy even in
those spiteful moments
of life that
it shares with
you. This poem
represents the hope
for a poetry
that doesn't turn
its back on
the audience, that
doesn't think it's
better than the reader,

that is committed
to poetry as a
popular form, like kite
flying and fly
fishing. This poem
belongs to no
school, has no
dogma. It follows
no fashion. It
says just what
it says. It's
real.

LET'S JUST SAY

Let's just say that every time you fall you never hit the ground

Let's just say that when the day ends the night refuses to come

Let's just say that if all else fails you at least you can count on that

Let's just say that a bird in the fist is better than a bird and a foot

Let's just say that the scarlet ambrosia of your innermost longing is
    the nectar of a god who never chooses to visit

Let's just say that if chance accords possibilities, melancholy
    postpones insomnia

Let's just say that sleep is the darker side of dreams

Let's just say that sometimes a rose is just a read flower

Let's just say that every step forward is also a step nowhere

Let's just say that the thirst for knowledge can only be quenched if
    one learns how to remain hungry

Let's just say that green is always a reflection of the idea of green

Let's just say that I encounter myself not in the mirror but in the manure

Let's just say that each door leads to another door

Let's just say that we think it before we see it or better we see it as we think it

Let's just say that a stone's throw might be a world away

Let's just say that love is neither here nor there

Let's just say that the girl is the mother of the woman

Let's just say that without disorder there can be no harmony

Let's just say that the aim is not to win but not to lose too bad

Let's just say that a knife in the back is better than a knife in the heart

Let's just say that between sleep and dreams is the reality behind reality

Let's just say that I am very weak and want to take a bath

Let's just say that the truth is somewhere between us

Let's just say that the top of a tower is not a good place to hide

Let's just say that mankind suffers its language

Let's just say that a bird cannot always be in flight

Let's just say that we're not far from where we would have been if
    we had lived better lives

Let's just say that pretty ugly is an aspiring oxymoron

Let's just say that if the sun is a rock burning in space then the earth
    is a shard hurtling from its designation

Let's just say that little is gained when nothing is lost

Let's just say that the lie of the mind is the light of perception

every lake has a house
& every house has a stove
& every stove has a pot
& every pot has a lid
& every lid has a handle
& every handle has a stem
& every stem has an edge
& every edge has a lining
& every lining has a margin
& every margin has a slit
& every slit has a slope
& every slope has a sum
& every sum has a factor
& every factor has a face
& every face has a thought
& every thought has a trap
& every trap has a door
& every door has a frame
& every frame has a roof
& every roof has a house
& every house has a lake

REPORT FROM LIBERTY STREET

I took a walk on Liberty Street today. Only it was not the same place as I had known before.

They thought they were going to heaven.

Large crowds surge inside the police barricades, stretching to get a glimpse of the colossal wreck. All that remains of the towers is two lattice facades standing upright amidst the rubble.

These vast and hollow trunks of steel are mocked by the impervious stare of the neighboring buildings that loom, intact, over the vacant center.

National Guard troops, many no more than teenagers, stand guard over us, the dazzled onlookers, the voyeurs of the disaster, shouting gruffly, yet with a strange and unexpectable kindness, "move on, move on, can't stop here."

We look on, perhaps not yet ready for despair, against our stronger instincts, which well up, boundless and bare.

They thought they were going to heaven.

There are so many troops that the metaphor of a war zone dissolves into an actuality.

Liberty Street is an occupied zone. We have occupied ourselves.

At Pier A on the Battery, there are two giant Apple "Think Different" ads with blown-up pictures of FDR and Eleanor Roosevelt, who preside over the scene with unflinching incomprehension.

Across the way, the sign on the almost completed "The Residences" at the Ritz-Carlton Downtown says: "Live in Legendary Luxury / Occupancy Fall 2001 / Spectacular Views."

They thought they were going to heaven.

At the checkpoint at Battery and West Street, four soldiers check the passes of every vehicle wanting to go north, and there is an endless stream of cars, busses (filled with workers), pickups, dumpsters, flatbeds. Even police in uniform show their IDs to the soldiers.

Battery Park has become a military staging ground, filled with jeeps and tents and soldiers in combat fatigues.

Because the park is closed, it's impossible to get to the Museum of Jewish Heritage: A Living Memorial to the Holocaust.

They thought they were going to heaven.

If downtown seems oddly detached, out of time or frozen in it, one of the most affecting sites is at the Times Square subway station. Around the cold tile columns in the central atrium of the station, people have put up dozens of homemade signs, each with a picture of someone. They say missing—not in the sense of "looking for," but rather, *feeling the loss*. The grief surrounding these columns is overwhelming and we look on as if hit by a wave of turbulence. Yet, despite the votive lights and candles in coffee mugs, which, remarkably, the transit authority has left undisturbed, these are secular shrines, in the most pedestrian and transient of all places in the city.

We are overwhelmed by explanations for things that, at the visceral level, can't be rationalized. Anyway not yet or not quite. Almost everyone I know is on their own particular edge, our preset worldviews snapping into place like a bulletproof shield on one of James Bond's cars. Only the presets aren't quite working, which makes for an interesting, if unhinging, shimmer at the edges of things.

We hear a lot of one song from 1918 by Irving Berlin, but not a hint of "How Deep Is the Ocean" or "Let's Face the Music and Dance" much less "You Can't Get a Man with Gun."

They thought they were going to heaven.

The movies keep playing in my head. Not *Towering Inferno*, but, do you remember in *Fail-Safe* where the President, played by Henry Fonda, launches a nuclear attack on New York to show the Russians that the U.S. attack on Moscow was a mistake? "Mr. Chairman," Fonda tells his Russian counterpart, "my wife is in New York today on a shopping trip and I have her on the phone right now. . . . Mr. Chairman, the phone has gone dead."

So it's almost no surprise to see someone with a T-shirt that says "What Part of Hatred Don't You Understand?"

I guess when two planes filled with passengers and tanked up with more fuel than it takes to get my moped from here to Mars and back hits skyscrapers with 20,000 people in them, it doesn't take a political scientist to know there's a lot of hate there.

The scary thing is that maybe what they hated most about America is not the bad part.

They thought they were going to heaven.

I find myself walking around making up arguments in my head, but when I try to write them down they dissolve in a flood of questions and misgivings. I value these questions, these misgivings, more than my analysis of the situation.

A new sport is checking not what stores have put up flags but which ones don't. Still, there is one Afghani joint in midtown that has no flag in sight. Stu and I head over to try out the lamb kebab.

In the media, there has been a good deal of flap over the use of the word "cowardly" to describe the people that commandeered the planes. I notice that on television this weekend the term of art is now "dastardly," though that is probably better applied to the villain in *Perils of Pauline*. Certainly these men were not timid nor did they turn and run like rabbits (the root of the word coward). But I think the fact that no one claimed responsibility has made it harder to react, which is part of the effect. The seeming cowardice is not in the action but in the refusal to take responsibility for the action; it's strategic rather than tactical.

They thought they were going to heaven.

"We got what we deserved," a shrill small voice inside some seems to be saying. But surely not *this* person, nor *this* one, not *this* one, nor *this* one.

Nor *this* one.

No one deserves to die this way. I think that goes without saying and yet I feel compelled to say it.

Even if "we" and "they" have felled many, too many (any is too many) in this way.

Not people willing to die for a cause (a fairly large group), nor even those willing to kill for a cause (also a fairly large group), but people willing to do *this* (a relatively small group).

They thought they were going to heaven.

Not cowards. Men of principle.

Oh yes, you may say, what's monstrous to one may be expediency to the other. I too have read Merleau-Ponty's *Humanism and Terror* and watched *Burn* and *The Battle of Algiers*. But that makes it no less monstrous.

They thought they were going to heaven.

Still, I don't think this form of monstrousness is only "out there." We have our own domestic product. We call it KKK or Timothy McVeigh, Lt. Calley or Dr. Strangelove.

They thought they were going to heaven.

Manhattan as transitional object: Both my parents were born and grew up in New York, their parents having found sanctuary here from places that proved . . . inhospitable. The ghosts of these transplanted souls, along with the ghosts of their many compatriots, haunt the Holy Warriors with a fury that drives them to seek refuge through the Gates of Hell.

The question isn't is art up to this but what else is art for?

They thought they were going to heaven.

"The lone and level sands stretch far away."

(SEPTEMBER 18–OCTOBER 1, 2001)

DIDN'T WE

Inch by inch, the paths breaking
into patches of blue and green

then black and brown, then
over the pass to the top of the

remotest interior, accustomed as
we are to torrential indifference

and beatific familiarity. "Look
up in the sky"—another ad for

vinyl tubing, pillow talk of
Whosits & Whatsits of Nob &

Kebob, Insley & Ufragious,
Ackabag & Boodalip. Bump right

along, pondering your song, while
roasting toast or grinding sand

or polishing the fabric softener
that stands between you and your

self. It was in 1943 and then again
one more time. Beat bird without a

feather to call its own, a miser who
lives on a pile of mylar, the studio

with the view of the studio, my
eclectric blinker maker, strapped

in for take off. NO FLOATING
ALLOWED. As quiet as

the steps to indelible vanishing.

IN A RESTLESS WORLD LIKE THIS IS

Not long ago, or maybe I dreamt it
Or made it up, or have suddenly lost
Track of its train in the hocus pocus
Of the dissolving days; no, if I bend
The turn around the corner, come at it
From all three sides at once, or bounce the ball
Against all manner of bleary-eyed fortune
Tellers—well, you can see for yourselves there's
Nothing up my sleeves, or notice even
Rocks occasionally break if enough
Pressure is applied. As far as you go

In one direction, all the further you'll
Have to go on before the way back has
Become totally indivisible.

BROKEN ENGLISH

What are you fighting for? The men move

decisively toward the execution chamber.
Joey takes aim but muffles his fire.

Overhead, the crescent moon cracks
the unbroken sky. A moth beats its wings
against the closed door—intransigence its

only lore. *What are you fighting for?* The sirens

cry wolf to the obedient masses who sway,
hysterical, in synch to the boys
on the back streets and the ladies of mourning.

Brushing up fate pixel by pixel, burnishing
dusk: the sum of entropy and elevation.

Tony takes it in his intestine, the sharp
pain in his body like ripples
in a sand dune, his face exquisitely detached

from any sign of the sensation. *What are*
you fighting for? The market plunges, savings

slip away like a greased pig in a taffy
pull. Sometimes the easiest thing is just to stop
thinking about it. Then it can just think you.

Depending on the angle of incline and the rate

of decomposition. Wives to each other, husbanding
the fear that feeds upon itself and its prey.
Doesn't that count for something, even

in these pitched accommodations?

What are you fighting for?

What are you fighting for?

LOST IN DROWNED BLISS

"Things are what they are, but we are never
what we are," she said as she wrapped the sand-
wich in plastic and tucked away the tears
in a flute.

"No it's things. They hourly
change before our eyes while we stay stuck in
who we are and where we have been."

"Things are
solid; we stumble, unglue, recombine."

"Or what we see is no more a part of
us than the baby who beckons from the
forest: we splinter in the void to catch
the light, then hail the sparks as paradise."

SUNSET AT QUAQUAVERSAL POINT

Intends by onset to skip over busted rhymes

Like a snail coats its belly with preconscious
Worm-envy on a plate engaging its met mat,
The gnat her pinky ring. One sting more

And the wave goes on periverbal autodeterrent

Chin by the tension fanner, two for five-
Fifty, *lend me a lip retractor*. Gosh, I'm
Gonna have to get you later, for now

Hold that thoughtlessness one more beat.

At the end of the day the pegs left standing
Form an arc around the moat till the rooster
Comes home with the mocking birds. Then

Fill the balloons with ludic runes and I will

Take her with mine left and lose her with mine
Right. Focus, then bend, the bear to the north
Wind, with sullen yet courageous élan. Surcease

Surcease—with a sneeze & a pleat & a pike, a

Spat & a spore, then no more. It's over &
Over & then it's not, as long as you never—
Well sometimes endeavor—as long as you

Never, as long as ever, say never nor ever again

Again.

A FLAME IN YOUR HEART

As slow as Methuselah and as old as

molasses, time passes but nobody ever
does anything about it—the soda water

at the club on Tuesday so much more fishy

than it used to be and the giant marmoset
in the bedroom wants more cookies and milk

before fading into memory's skipped disk.

Once you came to me in a shadow
and I don't know how to count the years

since, since counting is just the thing I

am learning not to do. Your bracelet
adorns your wrist like a knight in ardor

crying for a key to the tumbledown cabin

on the dunes. A bonnet repairs what
the billy goat embargoes—ocean of this

close and then again, until all the folds

are rounded into the bend. And we meet,
like actors in a made-for-TV mini-series,

at the end of a pier on a blind alley or

on a steamship or in a crowded piazza in
an unidentifiable Italian city that turns

out to be Bayonne. You're there in the final

scene and so am I but we don't recognize
each other because we've gone beyond

all that. Then the signal blasts with

unendurable music and we collapse into
the sound, into ourselves as make-believe

as any devout hugamug with a hankering

for infinite finitude: just a walk down the street
of the imaginary enclosure that becomes real

when shared.

CASTOR OIL

FOR EMMA

I went looking for my soul
In the song of a minor bird
But I could not find it there
Only the shadow of my thinking

The slow sea slaps slow water
On the ever farther shore
And myself pulled under
In the uneven humming
Of the still wavering warps

Tuneless, I wander, sundered
In lent blends of remote display
Until the bottom bottoms
In song-drenched light, cradled fold

THE BRICKLAYER'S ARMS

The bricklayer's arms are folded
into a knot. They crest across
a soft, rumpled body. The bricklayer's
arms—stolid and serene—are
out of joint with the quizzical
expression on the bricklayer's
face. The bricklayer's arms are
heavy and slump into a wingback
chair or threadbare sofa or
petulant carousel or dithyrambic
telescope. The bricklayer's arms
are molten, molded, mottled, mirrored,
mired in unclaimed histories
of insufficient estimation. The
bricklayer's arms float into
suspended air; glow, from an
inner right, in cascades of
slate, beacons of broken guile.
They are patched, poked, pummeled,
pent; averse to what has been,
oblivious to what will come.
The bricklayer's arms disappear
behind a cloud, then return
soft-focus, dusk-lit, gauzy,

tipped. The bricklayer's
arms refuse to tell the secret
of the bricklayer's house.
The bricklayer's arms abjure
exposure, encapsulate the brokered
seams of a riven dream, permissible
to a few, particular to none.
The bricklayer's arms court
detachment, reflect closure.
The bricklayer's arms arm themselves
against denial, parry promise, absorb
abjection. In the torn
time between never
and however, they dissolve
into the formaldehyde
of the heart's lost longing.
The bricklayer's arms found
a moment in the quicksilver
of immaterial solids:
perception as flight against charter,
ballast, cynosure. Falling into
shadow, the bricklayer's arms,
knees, neck, mouth, scalp,
shins, stomach, eyes,
blend into storm, cloud,
sand, crystal, fork, bend,
bay, sag, sigh, coast.

The bricklayer's arms are
charms of a parallel coexistence,
emblem of fused incalculability.
They lie low in
gummed silhouette, fly when
floored, sing in phrases to
the apparent drumbeat of incurious
imbrication. Solo flight marked of
bygones, tattered torrents, embers
of desuetude, the bricklayer's
arms peal a dull and somber tune.
The bricklayer's arms break
the silence of the bricklayer's
heart. The bricklayer's arms
are every bit as dense as the vague
mist that obscures the furnished
hold of the bricklayer's sight.
The bricklayer's arms
are the imperfect extension
of the bricklayer's thoughts.
No sea contains them, no
forest is as deep or sky as
boundless as the bounded
continent of the bricklayer's
arms. The bricklayer's arms
signify nothing, but never cease
to mean. Even the smallest

grain of sand tunes itself
to their contours. The bricklayer's
arms are empirical evidence of
the existence of the bricklayer's
soul. The bricklayer's arms are lost
in reverie's pale, sad, lush illusions;
snap back from the blind eye
or the quick retort to sail into
helplessness's velour paradise.
The bricklayer's arms are a figment
of the imagination of the bricklayer's
shoulders. Buoyed by incapacity,
sufficient to expectation, they are
the final destination of helpless
promises and muted aspirations.
The bricklayer's arms are blanched
in disavowal. Without preparation,
the bricklayer's arms enfold
the beached drives and mercurial
generosity the age remands.
Atlas of the forsaken mall
of final detours, harbinger
of ill-timed hums and oft-lorn
wings, the bricklayer's arms are
stamped by the artifice of token
and projection. The bricklayer's arms
cradle the soul of the lost world.

WHEREVER ANGELS GO

Oh, hey, buddy, can you spare me a dime?

I've been searching for you so long

Yeah, hey, sister, I ain't into no crime

Won't you show me the way to go home

Been a long time

Been a long time

Don't you know I've missed you so

Wherever angels go

I will take you there to glow

Oh, hey, buddy, will you spare me some time?

I've been searching for you so long

There is no climb

Makes no difference no mind

Wherever angels go

Oh, hey, buddy, can you spare me a dime?

I've been searching for you so long

Yeah, hey, sister, I ain't into no crime

Won't you show me the way to go home

Won't you show me the way to go home

War is the extension of prose by other means.

War is never having to say you're sorry.

War is the logical outcome of moral certainty.

War is conflict resolution for the aesthetically challenged.

War is a slow boat to heaven and an express train to hell.

War is either a failure to communicate or the most direct expression possible.

War is the first resort of scoundrels.

War is the legitimate right of the powerless to resist the violence of the powerful.

War is delusion just as peace is imaginary.

"War is beautiful because it combines the gunfire, the cannonades, the cease-fire, the scents, and the stench of putrefaction into a symphony."

"War is a thing that decides how it is to be done when it is to be done."

War is not a justification for the self-righteousness of the people who oppose it.

War is other people.

War is a five-mile hike in a one-mile cemetery.

War is nature's way of saying I told you so.

War is a fashioning of opportunity.

War is "a nipponized bit of the old sixth avenue el."

War is the reluctant foundation of justice and the unconscious guarantor of liberty.

War is the broken dream of the patriot.

War is the slow death of idealism.

War is realpolitik for the old and unmitigated realism for the young.

War is pragmatism with an inhuman face.

War is for the state what despair is for the person.

War is the end of the road for those who've lost their bearings.

War is a poem that is afraid of its shadow but furious in its course.

War is men turned into steel and women turned into ash.

War is never a reason for war but seldom a reason for anything else.

War is a casualty of truth just as truth is a casualty of war.

War is the redress of the naked.

War is the opiate of the politicians.

War is to compromise what morbidity is to mortality.

War is poetry without song.

War is the world's betrayal of the earth's plenitude.

War is like a gorilla at a teletype machine: not always the best choice
but sometimes the only one you've got.

War is a fever that feeds on blood.

War is never more than an extension of Thanatos.

War is the older generation's way of making up for the mistakes of
its youth.

War is moral, peace is ethical.

War is the ultimate entertainment.

War is resistance in the flesh.

War is capitalism's way of testing its limits.

War is an inevitable product of class struggle.

War is technology's uncle.

War is an excuse for lots of bad anti-war poetry.

War is the right of a people who are oppressed.

War is news that stays news.

War is the principal weapon of a revolution that can never be
achieved.

War pays for those who have nothing to lose.

War is Surrealism without art.

War is not won but survived.

War is two wrongs obliterating right.

War is the abandonment of reason in the name of principle.

War is sacrifice for an ideal.

War is the desecration of the real.

War is unjust even when it is just.

War is the revenge of the dead on the living.

War is revenge on the wrong person.

War is the cry of the child in black, the woman in red, and the man
in blue.

War is powerlessness.

War is raw.

War is the declared struggle of one state against another but it is also
the undeclared violence of the state against its own people.

War is no vice in the defense of liberty; appeasement is no virtue in
the pursuit of self-protection.

War is tyranny's greatest foe.

War is tyranny's greatest friend.

War is the solution; but what is the problem?

War is a horse that bridles its rider.

War is the inadequate symbol of human society.

War is the best way to stoke the dying embers of ancient enmities.

War is a battle for the hearts and minds of the heartless and mindless.

War is history as told by the victors.

War is the death of civilization in the pursuit of civilization.

War is the end justifying the meanness.

War is an SUV for every soccer Pop and social Mom.

War is made by the rich and paid by the poor.

War is the quality TV alternative to *You Still Don't Know Jacko:
Cookin' with Michael* and *Fear Factor: How to Marry a Bachelorette.*

War is not a metaphor.

War is not ironic.

War is sincerity in serial motion.

War is a game of chess etched in flesh.

War is tactical violence for strategic dominance.

War is international engagement to cover domestic indifference.

War is the devil in overdrive.

War is our only hope.

War is our inheritance.

War is our patrimony.

War is our right.

War is our obligation.

War is justified only when it stops war.

War isn't over even when it's over.

War is "over here."

War is the answer.

War is here.

War is this.

War is now.

War is us.

THE BALLAD OF THE GIRLY MAN

FOR FELIX

The truth is hidden in a veil of tears
The scabs of the mourners grow thick with fear

A democracy once proposed
Is slimmed and grimed again
By men with brute design
Who prefer hate to rime

Complexity's a four-letter word
For those who count by nots and haves
Who revile the facts of Darwin
To worship the truth according to Halliburton

The truth is hidden in a veil of tears
The scabs of the mourners grow thick with fear

Thugs from hell have taken freedom's store
The rich get richer, the poor die quicker
& the only god that sanctions that
Is no god at all but rhetorical crap

So be a girly man
& take a gurly stand

Sing a gurly song
& dance with a girly sarong

Poetry will never win the war on terror
But neither will error abetted by error

We girly men are not afraid
Of uncertainty or reason or interdependence
We think before we fight, then think some more
Proclaim our faith in listening, in art, in compromise

So be a girly man
& sing this gurly song
Sissies & proud
That we would never lie our way to war

The girly men killed christ
So the platinum DVD says
The Jews & blacks & gays
Are still standing in the way

We're sorry we killed your god
A long, long time ago
But each dead soldier in Iraq
Kills the god inside, the god that's still not dead.

The truth is hidden in a veil of tears
The scabs of the mourners grow thick with fear

So be a girly man
& sing a gurly song
Take a gurly stand
& dance with a girly sarong

Thugs from hell have taken freedom's store
The rich get richer, the poor die quicker
& the only god that sanctions that
Is no god at all but rhetorical crap

So be a girly man
& sing this gurly song
Sissies & proud
That we would never lie our way to war

The scabs of the mourners grow thick with fear
The truth is hidden in a veil of tears

ENVOI

ALL THE WHISKEY IN HEAVEN

Not for all the whiskey in heaven
Not for all the flies in Vermont
Not for all the tears in the basement
Not for a million trips to Mars

Not if you paid me in diamonds
Not if you paid me in pearls
Not if you gave me your pinky ring
Not if you gave me your curls

Not for all the fire in hell
Not for all the blue in the sky
Not for an empire of my own
Not even for peace of mind

No, never, I'll never stop loving you
Not till my heart beats its last
And even then in my words and my songs
I will love you all over again

ACKNOWLEDGMENTS AND NOTES

I am grateful to Marjorie Perloff for her suggestions on the selection and support for this project. I very much appreciate cogent advice from Jerome McGann, Susan Howe, Peter Gizzi, Tan Lin, Wystan Curnow, Jonathan Galassi, and Susan Bee.

The poems in this book are reprinted, with the permission of the author and thanks to the publishers, from the following books, with special thanks to Douglas Messerli (Sun & Moon Press), James Sherry (Roof Books), and Alan Thomas (University of Chicago Press).

> *Asylums* (New York: Asylums Press, 1975). "Asylum" is collaged from Erving Goffman's *Asylums: Essays on the Social Situation of Mental Patients and Other Inmates.*
>
> *Shade* (College Park, Md.: Sun & Moon Press, 1978)
>
> *Senses of Responsibility* (Berkeley: Tuumba Press, 1979; repr. Providence: Paradigm Press, 1989)
>
> *Poetic Justice* (Baltimore: Pod Books, 1979). "Lift Off" is a transcription from the correction tape of an IBM Selectric typewriter.
>
> *Controlling Interests* (New York: Roof Books, 1980; repr. 2008)
>
> *Stigma* (Barrytown, N.Y.: Station Hill Press, 1981)
>
> *Resistance* (Windsor, Vt.: Awede Press, 1983)
>
> *Islets/Irritations* (New York: Jordan Davies, 1983; repr. New York: Roof Books, 1992, 2008)
>
> *The Sophist* (Los Angeles: Sun & Moon Press, 1987; repr. Cambridge, U.K.: Salt Publishing, 2004). "Dysraphism" is a dysfunctional fusion of embryonic parts (*raph* means seam); *rhaptein*, to sew, is a root for *rhapsody*, songs sewn together.
>
> *The Absent Father in* Dumbo (Canary Islands, Spain: Zasterle, 1990)

Rough Trades (Los Angeles: Sun & Moon Press, 1991)

Dark City (Los Angeles: Sun & Moon Press, 1994). "The Influence of Kinship Patterns . . ." was written for a collection of essays on John Ashbery.

My Way: Speeches and Poems (Chicago: University of Chicago Press, 1999). "A Defence of Poetry," which is made up of proliferated typographical errors, is a reply to "Making (non)sense of postmodernist poetry" by Brian McHale. "Gertrude and Ludwig's Great Adventure" is dedicated to Marjorie Perloff, whose name at birth was Gabriele Mintz. "A Test of Poetry" is based on a letter from my friend Ziquing Zhang, who translated poems from *Rough Trades* and *The Sophist* for *Selected Language Poems* (Chengdu, China: Sichuan Literature and Art Publishing House, 1993); quotations from the poems are italicized. "This Line" and "Riddle" are from the serial poem "Republic of Reality."

Residual Rubbernecking (2000). First published in *Republics of Reality: 1975–1995* (Los Angeles: Sun & Moon Press, 2000).

With Strings (Chicago: University of Chicago Press, 2001)

Let's Just Say (Tucson, Ariz.: Chax Press, 2003). Written in the summer of 2001. Collected in *Girly Man*.

World on Fire (Vancouver: Nomados, 2004). Written in the summer of 2002. Collected in *Girly Man*.

Some of These Daze, with drawings by Mimi Gross (New York: Granary Books, 2005). Written in the fall of 2001; excerpted in the Granary book, complete work in *Girly Man*. "Report from Liberty Street" appears in this book according to the date of composition rather than book publication.

Girly Man (Chicago: University of Chicago Press, 2006)

"All the Whiskey in Heaven" was originally published in *The Nation* (2008).